ON
FRIENDSHIP
AND
OLD AGE

ON FRIENDSHIP AND OLD AGE

MARCUS TULLIUS CICERO

TRANSLATED BY
E.S. SHUCKBURGH

Disclaimer
Throughout the text readers may find that some of the language used
and sentiments expressed are offensive and unacceptable by today's standards.
These reflect the attitudes and usage common at the time the book was written.
In no way do they reflect the attitude of the publishers.

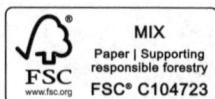

MIX
Paper | Supporting
responsible forestry
FSC® C104723
www.fsc.org

CONTENTS

INTRODUCTION

MARCUS TULLIUS CICERO, born on 3 January 106 BC, was an important ancient Roman orator, lawyer and politician. Raised in a wealthy family, he was trained from an early age in the Greek philosophical and rhetorical traditions which would influence his later writings. During his life and political career as a Roman senator and consul (chief-magistrate), Cicero saw the rise and fall of Julius Caesar as well as the transformation of the Roman Republic into the Roman Empire. He is still appreciated today for his extensive literary contributions, and his speeches, letters and essays remain one of the most renowned collections of historical, political and philosophical work in all of classical antiquity. His philosophical writings especially influenced Western civilization during the Renaissance and Enlightenment.

It was while Cicero was consul that the Catiline conspiracy – an attempt to overthrow the government – failed and he allegedly drove Catiline from Rome with his famous *Catilinarian Orations* – four speeches considered prime examples of his rhetorical style. Following this upheaval, Cicero executed four traitors without trial, which later led to his year-long exile from Rome. Upon his return, he struggled to find his way back into politics and instead focused on his literary works covering a wide array of subjects.

Aged 63, Cicero wrote his essay 'On Old Age' in 44 BC, originally titled '*Cato Maior de Senectute*' ('Cato the Elder on Old Age'), which discusses the matters of aging and death. This entirely fictional dialogue between Cato the Elder and two younger men is typical of Greek and Roman philosophical writings and therefore gives Cicero's reflections greater importance. His blend of personal and historical ideas on how old age is not only tolerable but can be comfortable is still relevant today and has remained popular due to the essay's clear and elegant language. Also included is the treatise 'On Friendship' written in 44 BC and considered to be a deeply insightful dialogue on the nature of friendship and role it plays in one's life.

After Caesar's assassination in 44 BC, Cicero supported Octavian over Mark Antony in the ensuing power struggle, attacking the latter in several speeches and declaring him an enemy of the state. However, tragically, Cicero's vocality eventually led to his downfall when he himself was proscribed an enemy after Octavian and Antony reconciled. He was captured and executed on 7 December 43 BC, while attempting to flee from Rome.

INTRODUCTORY NOTE

MARCUS TULLIUS CICERO, the greatest of Roman orators and the chief master of Latin prose style, was born at Arpinum, Jan. 3, 106 BC. His father, who was a man of property and belonged to the class of the 'Knights', moved to Rome when Cicero was a child; and the future statesman received an elaborate education in rhetoric, law, and philosophy, studying and practising under some of the most noted teachers of the time. He began his career as an advocate at the age of twenty-five, and almost immediately came to be recognized not only as a man of brilliant talents but also as a courageous upholder of justice in the face of grave political danger. After two years of practice he left Rome to travel in Greece and Asia, taking all the opportunities that offered to study his art under distinguished masters. He returned to Rome greatly improved in health and in professional skill, and in 76 BC. was elected to the office of quaestor. He was assigned to the province of Lilybaeum in Sicily, and the vigour and justice of his administration earned him the gratitude of the inhabitants. It was at their request that he undertook in 70 BC the Prosecution of Verres, who as praetor had subjected the Sicilians to incredible extortion and oppression; and his successful conduct of this case, which ended in the conviction and banishment of Verres, may be said to have launched him on his political career. He became aedile in the same year, in 67 BC praetor, and in 64 BC was elected consul by a large majority. The most important event of the year of his consulship was the conspiracy of Catiline. This notorious criminal of patrician rank had conspired with a number of others, many of them young men of high birth but dissipated character, to seize the chief offices of the state, and to extricate themselves from the pecuniary and other difficulties that had resulted from their excesses, by the wholesale plunder of the city. The plot was unmasked by the vigilance of Cicero, five of the traitors were summarily executed, and in the overthrow of the army that had been gathered in their support Catiline himself perished. Cicero regarded himself as the saviour of his country, and his country for the moment seemed to give grateful assent.

But reverses were at hand. During the existence of the political combination of Pompey, Caesar, and Crassus, known as the first triumvirate, P. Clodius, an enemy of Cicero's, proposed a law banishing 'any one who had put Roman citizens to death without trial'. This was aimed at Cicero on account of his share in the Catiline affair, and in March 58 BC, he left Rome. The same day a law was passed by which he was banished by name, and his property was plundered and destroyed, a temple to Liberty being erected on the site of his house in the city.

During his exile Cicero's manliness to some extent deserted him. He drifted from place to place, seeking the protection of officials against assassination, writing letters urging his supporters to agitate for his recall, sometimes accusing them of lukewarmness and even treachery, bemoaning the ingratitude of his country or regretting the course of action that had led to his outlawry, and suffering from extreme depression over his separation from his wife and children and the wreck of his political ambitions. Finally in August 57 BC, the decree for his restoration was passed, and he returned to Rome the next month, being received with immense popular enthusiasm. During the next few years the renewal of the understanding among the triumvirs shut Cicero out from any leading part in politics, and he resumed his activity in the law-courts, his most important case being, perhaps, the defence of Milo for the murder of Clodius, Cicero's most troublesome enemy. This oration, in the revised form in which it has come down to us, is ranked as among the finest specimens of the art of the orator, though in its original form it failed to secure Milo's acquittal. Meantime, Cicero was also devoting much time to literary composition, and his letters show great dejection over the political situation, and a somewhat wavering attitude towards the various parties in the state. In 55 BC he went to Cilicia in Asia Minor as proconsul, an office which he administered with efficiency and integrity in civil affairs and with success in military. He returned to Italy at the end of the following year, and he was publicly thanked by the senate for his services, but disappointed in his hopes for a triumph. The war for supremacy between Caesar and Pompey which had for some time been gradually growing more certain, broke out in 49 BC, when Caesar led his army across the Rubicon, and Cicero after much irresolution threw in his lot with Pompey, who was overthrown the next year in the battle of Pharsalus and later murdered in Egypt.

Cicero returned to Italy, where Caesar treated him magnanimously, and for some time he devoted himself to philosophical and rhetorical writing. In 46 BC he divorced his wife Terentia, to whom he had been married for thirty years, and married the young and wealthy Publilia in order to relieve himself from financial difficulties; but her also he shortly divorced. Caesar, who had now become supreme in Rome, was assassinated in 44 BC, and though Cicero was not a sharer in the conspiracy, he seems to have approved the deed. In the confusion which followed he supported the cause of the conspirators against Antony; and when finally the triumvirate of Antony, Octavius, and Lepidus was established, Cicero was included among the proscribed, and on December 7, 43 BC, he was killed by agents of Antony. His head and hand were cut off and exhibited at Rome.

The most important orations of the last months of his life were the fourteen 'Philippics' delivered against Antony, and the price of this enmity he paid with his life.

To his contemporaries Cicero was primarily the great forensic and political orator of his time, and the fifty-eight speeches which have come down to us bear testimony to the skill, wit, eloquence, and passion which gave him his pre-eminence. But these speeches of necessity deal with the minute details of the occasions which called them forth, and so require for their appreciation a full knowledge of the history, political and personal, of the time. The letters, on the other hand, are less elaborate both in style and in the handling of current events, while they serve to reveal his personality, and to throw light upon Roman life in the last days of the Republic in an extremely vivid fashion.

Cicero as a man, in spite of his self-importance, the vacillation of his political conduct in desperate crises, and the whining despondency of his times of adversity, stands out as at bottom a patriotic Roman of substantial honesty, who gave his life to check the inevitable fall of the commonwealth to which he was devoted. The evils which were undermining the Republic bear so many striking resemblances to those which threaten the civic and national life of America that the interest of the period is by no means merely historical.

As a philosopher, Cicero's most important function was to make his countrymen familiar with the main schools of Greek thought. Much of this writing is thus of secondary interest to us in comparison with his originals, but in the fields of religious theory and of the application of philosophy to life he made important first-hand contributions. From these works have been selected the two treatises, *On Old Age* and *On Friendship*, which have proved of most permanent and widespread interest to posterity, and which give a clear impression of the way in which a high-minded Roman thought about some of the main problems of human life.

ON FRIENDSHIP

THE augur Quintus Mucius Scaevola used to recount a number of stories about his father-in-law, Gaius Laelius, accurately remembered and charmingly told; and whenever he talked about him always gave him the title of 'the wise' without any hesitation. I had been introduced by my father to Scaevola as soon as I had assumed the *toga virilis*, and I took advantage of the introduction never to quit the venerable man's side as long as I was able to stay and he was spared to us. The consequence was that I committed to memory many disquisitions of his, as well as many short pointed apophthegms, and, in short, took as much advantage of his wisdom as I could. When he died, I attached myself to Scaevola the Pontifex, whom I may venture to call quite the most distinguished of our countrymen for ability and uprightness. But of this latter I shall take other occasions to speak. To return to Scaevola the augur. Among many other occasions I particularly remember one. He was sitting on a semicircular garden-bench, as was his custom, when I and a very few intimate friends were there, and he chanced to turn the conversation upon a subject which about that time was in many people's mouths. You must remember,

Atticus, for you were very intimate with Publius Sulpicius, what expressions of astonishment, or even indignation, were called forth by his mortal quarrel, as tribune, with the consul Quintus Pompeius, with whom he had formerly lived on terms of the closest intimacy and affection. Well, on this occasion, happening to mention this particular circumstance, Scaevola detailed to us a discourse of Laelius on friendship delivered to himself and Laelius's other son-in-law Gaius Fannius, son of Marcus Fannius, a few days after the death of Africanus. The points of that discussion I committed to memory, and have arranged them in this book at my own discretion. For I have brought the speakers, as it were, personally on to my stage to prevent the constant 'said I' and 'said he' of a narrative, and to give the discourse the air of being orally delivered in our hearing.

You have often urged me to write something on Friendship, and I quite acknowledged that the subject seemed one worth everybody's investigation, and specially suited to the close intimacy that has existed between you and me. Accordingly I was quite ready to benefit the public at your request.

As to the *dramatis personae* in the treatise *On Old Age*, which I dedicated to you, I introduced Cato as chief speaker. No one, I thought, could with greater propriety speak on old age than one who had been an old man longer than any one else, and had been exceptionally vigorous in his old age. Similarly, having learnt from tradition that of all friendships that between Gaius Laelius and Publius Scipio was the most remarkable, I thought Laelius was just the person to support the chief part in a discussion on friendship which Scaevola remembered him to have actually taken.

Moreover, a discussion of this sort gains somehow in weight from the authority of men of ancient days, especially if they happen to have been distinguished. So it comes about that in reading over what I have myself written I have a feeling at times that it is actually Cato that is speaking, not I.

Finally, as I sent the former essay to you as a gift from one old man to another, so I have dedicated this *On Friendship* as a most affectionate friend to his friend. In the former Cato spoke, who was the oldest and wisest man of his day; in this Laelius speaks on friendship – Laelius, who was at once a wise man (that was the title given him) and eminent for his famous friendship. Please forget me for a while; imagine Laelius to be speaking.

Gaius Fannius and Quintus Mucius come to call on their father-in-law after the death of Africanus. They start the subject; Laelius answers them. And the whole essay on friendship is his. In reading it you will recognize a picture of yourself.

***

2. *Fannius.* You are quite right, Laelius! There never was a better or more illustrious character than Africanus. But you should consider that at the present moment all eyes are on you. Everybody calls you 'the wise' *par excellence*, and thinks you so. The same mark of respect was lately paid Cato, and we know that in the last generation Lucius Atilius was called 'the wise'. But in both cases the word was applied with a certain difference. Atilius was so called from his reputation as a jurist; Cato got the name as a kind of honorary title and in extreme old age because of his

varied experience of affairs, and his reputation for foresight and firmness, and the sagacity of the opinions which he delivered in senate and forum. You, however, are regarded as wise in a somewhat different sense – not alone on account of natural ability and character, but also from your industry and learning; and not in the sense in which the vulgar, but that in which scholars, give that title. In this sense we do not read of any one being called wise in Greece except one man at Athens; and he, to be sure, had been declared by the oracle of Apollo also to be 'the supremely wise man'. For those who commonly go by the name of the Seven Sages are not admitted into the category of the wise by fastidious critics. Your wisdom people believe to consist in this, that you look upon yourself as self-sufficing and regard the changes and chances of mortal life as powerless to affect your virtue. Accordingly they are always asking me, and doubtless also our Scaevola here, how you bear the death of Africanus. This curiosity has been the more excited from the fact that on the Nones of this month, when we augurs met as usual in the suburban villa of Decimus Brutus for consultation, you were not present, though it had always been your habit to keep that appointment and perform that duty with the utmost punctuality.

Scaevola. Yes, indeed, Laelius, I am often asked the question mentioned by Fannius. But I answer in accordance with what I have observed: I say that you bear in a reasonable manner the grief which you have sustained in the death of one who was at once a man of the most illustrious character and a very dear friend. That of course you could not but be affected – anything else would have been wholly unnatural in a man of your gentle nature – but that the cause of your non-attendance at our college meeting was illness, not melancholy.

Laelius. Thanks, Scaevola! You are quite right; you spoke the exact truth. For in fact I had no right to allow myself to be withdrawn from a duty which I had regularly performed, as long as I was well, by any personal misfortune; nor do I think that anything that can happen will cause a man of principle to intermit a duty. As for your telling me, Fannius, of the honourable appellation given me (an appellation to which I do not recognize my title, and to which I make no claim), you doubtless act from feelings of affection; but I must say that you seem to me to do less than justice to Cato. If any one was ever 'wise' – of which I have my doubts – he was. Putting aside everything else, consider how he bore his son's death! I had not forgotten Paulus; I had seen with my own eyes Gallus. But they lost their sons when mere children; Cato his when he was a full-grown man with an assured reputation. Do not therefore be in a hurry to reckon as Cato's superior even that same famous personage whom Apollo, as you say, declared to be 'the wisest'. Remember the former's reputation rests on deeds, the latter's on words.

3. Now, as far as I am concerned (I speak to both of you now), believe me the case stands thus: if I were to say that I am not affected by regret for Scipio, I must leave the philosophers to justify my conduct, but in point of fact I should be telling a lie. Affected of course I am by the loss of a friend as I think there will never be again, such as I

can fearlessly say there never was before. But I stand in no need of medicine. I can find my own consolation, and it consists chiefly in my being free from the mistaken notion which generally causes pain at the departure of friends. To Scipio I am convinced no evil has befallen: mine is the disaster, if disaster there be; and to be severely distressed at one's own misfortunes does not show that you love your friend, but that you love yourself.

As for him, who can say that all is not more than well? For, unless he had taken the fancy to wish for immortality, the last thing of which he ever thought, what is there for which mortal man may wish that he did not attain? In his early manhood he more than justified by extraordinary personal courage the hopes which his fellow-citizens had conceived of him as a child. He never was a candidate for the consulship, yet was elected consul twice: the first time before the legal age; the second at a time which, as far as he was concerned, was soon enough, but was near being too late for the interests of the State. By the overthrow of two cities which were the most bitter enemies of our Empire, he put an end not only to the wars then raging, but also to the possibility of others in the future. What need to mention the exquisite grace of his manners, his dutiful devotion to his mother, his generosity to his sisters, his liberality to his relations, the integrity of his conduct to every one? You know all this already. Finally, the estimation in which his fellow-citizens held him has been shown by the signs of mourning which accompanied his obsequies. What could such a man have gained by the addition of a few years? Though age need not be a burden – as I remember Cato arguing in the presence of myself and Scipio two years before he died – yet it cannot but take away the vigour and freshness which Scipio was still enjoying. We may conclude therefore that his life, from the good fortune which had attended him and the glory he had obtained, was so circumstanced that it could not be bettered, while the suddenness of his death saved him the sensation of dying. As to the manner of his death it is difficult to speak; you see what people suspect. Thus much, however, I may say: Scipio in his lifetime saw many days of supreme triumph and exultation, but none more magnificent than his last, on which, upon the rising of the Senate, he was escorted by the senators and the people of Rome, by the allies, and by the Latins, to his own door. From such an elevation of popular esteem the next step seems naturally to be an ascent to the gods above, rather than a descent to Hades.

4. For I am not one of these modern philosophers who maintain that our souls perish with our bodies, and that death ends all. With me ancient opinion has more weight: whether it be that of our own ancestors, who attributed such solemn observances to the dead, as they plainly would not have done if they had believed them to be wholly annihilated; or that of the philosophers who once visited this country, and who by their maxims and doctrines educated Magna Graecia, which at that time was in a flourishing condition, though it has now been ruined; or that of the man who was declared by Apollo's oracle to be 'most wise', and who used to teach without the variation which is to be found in most philosophers that 'the souls of men are divine, and that when they have quitted the body a return to heaven is open to them, least difficult to

those who have been most virtuous and just'. This opinion was shared by Scipio. Only a few days before his death – as though he had a presentiment of what was coming – he discoursed for three days on the state of the republic. The company consisted of Philus and Manlius and several others, and I had brought you, Scaevola, along with me. The last part of his discourse referred principally to the immortality of the soul; for he told us what he had heard from the elder Africanus in a dream. Now if it be true that in proportion to a man's goodness the escape from what may be called the prison and bonds of the flesh is easiest, whom can we imagine to have had an easier voyage to the gods than Scipio? I am disposed to think, therefore, that in his case mourning would be a sign of envy rather than of friendship. If, however, the truth rather is that the body and soul perish together, and that no sensation remains, then though there is nothing good in death, at least there is nothing bad. Remove sensation, and a man is exactly as though he had never been born; and yet that this man was born is a joy to me, and will be a subject of rejoicing to this State to its last hour.

Wherefore, as I said before, all is as well as possible with him. Not so with me; for as I entered life before him, it would have been fairer for me to leave it also before him. Yet such is the pleasure I take in recalling our friendship, that I look upon my life as having been a happy one because I have spent it with Scipio. With him I was associated in public and private business; with him I lived in Rome and served abroad; and between us there was the most complete harmony in our tastes, our pursuits, and our sentiments, which is the true secret of friendship. It is not

ON FRIENDSHIP AND OLD AGE

therefore in that reputation for wisdom mentioned just now by Fannius – especially as it happens to be groundless – that I find my happiness so much, as in the hope that the memory of our friendship will be lasting. What makes me care the more about this is the fact that in all history there are scarcely three or four pairs of friends on record; and it is classed with them that I cherish a hope of the friendship of Scipio and Laelius being known to posterity.

Fannius. Of course that must be so, Laelius. But since you have mentioned the word friendship, and we are at leisure, you would be doing me a great kindness, and I expect Scaevola also, if you would do as it is your habit to do when asked questions on other subjects, and tell us your sentiments about friendship, its nature, and the rules to be observed in regard to it.

Scaevola. I shall of course be delighted. Fannius has anticipated the very request I was about to make. So you will be doing us both a great favour.

5. *Laelius.* I should certainly have no objection if I felt confidence in myself. For the theme is a noble one, and we are (as Fannius has said) at leisure. But who am I? And what ability have I? What you propose is all very well for professional philosophers, who are used, particularly if Greeks, to have the subject for discussion proposed to them on the spur of the moment. It is a task of considerable difficulty, and requires no little practice. Therefore for a set discourse on friendship you must go, I think, to professional lecturers. All I can do is to urge on you to regard friendship

as the greatest thing in the world; for there is nothing which so fits in with our nature, or is so exactly what we want in prosperity or adversity.

But I must at the very beginning lay down this principle: *friendship can only exist between good men.* I do not, however, press this too closely, like the philosophers who push their definitions to a superfluous accuracy. They have truth on their side, perhaps, but it is of no practical advantage. Those, I mean, who say that no one but the 'wise' is 'good'. Granted, by all means. But the 'wisdom' they mean is one to which no mortal ever yet attained. We must concern ourselves with the facts of everyday life as we find it – not imaginary and ideal perfections. Even Gaius Fannius, Manius Curius, and Tiberius Coruncanius, whom our ancestors decided to be 'wise', I could never declare to be so according to their standard. Let them, then, keep this word 'wisdom' to themselves. Everybody is irritated by it; no one understands what it means. Let them but grant that the men I mentioned were 'good'. No, they won't do that either. No one but the 'wise' can be allowed that title, say they. Well, then, let us dismiss them and manage as best we may with our own poor mother wit, as the phrase is.

We mean then by the 'good' *those whose actions and lives leave no question as to their honour, purity, equity, and liberality; who are free from greed, lust, and violence; and who have the courage of their convictions.* The men I have just named may serve as examples. Such men as these being generally accounted 'good', let us agree to call them so, on the ground that to the best of human ability they follow nature as the most perfect guide to a good life.

Now this truth seems clear to me, that nature has so

formed us that a certain tie unites us all, but that this tie becomes stronger from proximity. So it is that fellow-citizens are preferred in our affections to foreigners, relations to strangers; for in their case Nature herself has caused a kind of friendship to exist, though it is one which lacks some of the elements of permanence. Friendship excels relationship in this, that whereas you may eliminate affection from relationship, you cannot do so from friendship. Without it relationship still exists in name, friendship does not. You may best understand this friendship by considering that, whereas the merely natural ties uniting the human race are indefinite, this one is so concentrated, and confined to so narrow a sphere, that affection is ever shared by two persons only or at most by a few.

6. Now friendship may be thus defined: *a complete accord on all subjects human and divine, joined with mutual goodwill and affection*. And with the exception of wisdom, I am inclined to think nothing better than this has been given to man by the immortal gods. There are people who give the palm to riches or to good health, or to power and office, many even to sensual pleasures. This last is the ideal of brute beasts; and of the others we may say that they are frail and uncertain, and depend less on our own prudence than on the caprice of fortune. Then there are those who find the 'chief good' in virtue. Well, that is a noble doctrine. But the very virtue they talk of is the parent and preserver of friendship, and without it friendship cannot possibly exist.

Let us, I repeat, use the word virtue in the ordinary acceptation and meaning of the term, and do not let us define it in high-flown language. Let us account as good the persons usually considered so, such as Paulus, Cato, Gallus, Scipio, and Philus. Such men as these are good enough for everyday life; and we need not trouble ourselves about those ideal characters which are nowhere to be met with.

Well, between men like these the advantages of friendship are almost more than I can say. To begin with, how can life be worth living, to use the words of Ennius, which lacks that repose which is to be found in the mutual good-will of a friend? What can be more delightful than to have some one to whom you can say everything with the same absolute confidence as to yourself? Is not prosperity robbed of half its value if you have no one to share your joy? On the other hand, misfortunes would be hard to bear if there were not some one to feel them even more acutely than yourself. In a word, other objects of ambition serve for particular ends – riches for use, power for securing homage, office for reputation, pleasure for enjoyment, health for freedom from pain and the full use of the functions of the body. But friendship embraces innumerable advantages. Turn which way you please, you will find it at hand. It is everywhere; and yet never out of place, never unwelcome. Fire and water themselves, to use a common expression, are not of more universal use than friendship. I am not now speaking of the common or modified form of it, though even that is a source of pleasure and profit, but of that true and complete friendship which existed between the select few who are known to fame. Such friendship enhances prosperity, and relieves adversity of its burden by halving and sharing it.

7. And great and numerous as are the blessings of friendship, this certainly is the sovereign one, that it gives us bright hopes for the future and forbids weakness and despair. In the face of a true friend a man sees as it were a second self. So that where his friend is he is; if his friend be rich, he is not poor; though he be weak, his friend's strength is his; and in his friend's life he enjoys a second life after his own is finished. This last is perhaps the most difficult to conceive. But such is the effect of the respect, the loving remembrance, and the regret of friends which follow us to the grave. While they take the sting out of death, they add a glory to the life of the survivors. Nay, if you eliminate from nature the tie of affection, there will be an end of house and city, nor will so much as the cultivation of the soil be left. If you don't see the virtue of friendship and harmony, you may learn it by observing the effects of quarrels and feuds. Was any family ever so well established, any State so firmly settled, as to be beyond the reach of utter destruction from animosities and factions? This may teach you the immense advantage of friendship.

They say that a certain philosopher of Agrigentum, in a Greek poem, pronounced with the authority of an oracle the doctrine that whatever in nature and the universe was unchangeable was so in virtue of the binding force of friendship; whatever was changeable was so by the solvent power of discord. And indeed this is a truth which everybody understands and practically attests by experience. For if any marked instance of loyal friendship in confronting or sharing danger comes to light, every one applauds it to the echo. What cheers there were, for instance, all over the theatre at a passage in the new play of my friend and guest Pacuvius; where the king, not knowing which of the two was Orestes, Pylades declared himself to be Orestes, that he might die in his stead, while the real Orestes kept on asserting that it was he. The audience rose *en masse* and clapped their hands. And this was at an incident in fiction: what would they have done, must we suppose, if it had been in real life? You can easily see what a natural feeling it is, when men who would not have had the resolution to act thus themselves, shewed how right they thought it in another.

I don't think I have any more to say about friendship. If there is any more, and I have no doubt there is much, you must, if you care to do so, consult those who profess to discuss such matters.

Fannius. We would rather apply to you. Yet I have often consulted such persons, and have heard what they had to say with a certain satisfaction. But in your discourse one somehow feels that there is a different strain.

Scaevola. You would have said that still more, Fannius, if you had been present the other day in Scipio's pleasure-grounds when we had the discussion about the State. How splendidly he stood up for justice against Philus's elaborate speech.

Fannius. Ah! it was naturally easy for the justest of men to stand up for justice.

Scaevola. Well, then, what about friendship? Who could discourse on it more easily than the man whose chief glory is a friendship maintained with the most absolute fidelity, constancy, and integrity?

8. *Laelius*. Now you are really using force. It makes no difference what kind of force you use: force it is. For it is neither easy nor right to refuse a wish of my sons-in-law, particularly when the wish is a creditable one in itself.

Well, then, it has very often occurred to me when thinking about friendship, that the chief point to be considered was this: is it weakness and want of means that make friendship desired? I mean, is its object an interchange of good offices, so that each may give that in which he is strong, and receive that in which he is weak? Or is it not rather true that, although this is an advantage naturally belonging to friendship, yet its original cause is quite other, prior in time, more noble in character, and springing more directly from our nature itself? The Latin word for friendship – *amicitia* – is derived from that for love – *amor*; and love is certainly the prime mover in contracting mutual affection. For as to material advantages, it often happens that those are obtained even by men who are courted by a mere show of friendship and treated with respect from interested motives. But friendship by its nature admits of no feigning, no pretence: as far as it goes it is both genuine and spontaneous. Therefore I gather that friendship springs from a natural impulse rather than a wish for help: from an inclination of the heart, combined with a certain instinctive feeling of love, rather than from a deliberate calculation of the material advantage it was likely to confer. The strength of this feeling you may notice in certain animals. They show such love to their offspring for a certain period, and are so beloved by them, that they clearly have a share in this natural, instinctive affection. But of course it is more evident in the case of man: first, in the natural affection between children and their parents, an affection which only shocking wickedness can sunder; and next, when the passion of love has attained to a like strength – on our finding, that is, some one person with whose character and nature we are in full sympathy, because we think that we perceive in him what I may call the beacon-light of virtue. For nothing inspires love, nothing conciliates affection, like virtue. Why, in a certain sense we may be said to feel affection even for men we have never seen, owing to their honesty and virtue. Who, for instance, fails to dwell on the memory of Gaius Fabricius and Manius Curius with some affection and warmth of feeling, though he has never seen them? Or who but loathes Tarquinius Superbus, Spurius Cassius, Spurius Maelius? We have fought for empire in Italy with two great generals, Pyrrhus and Hannibal. For the former, owing to his probity, we entertain no great feelings of enmity: the latter, owing to his cruelty, our country has detested and always will detest.

9. Now, if the attraction of probity is so great that we can love it not only in those whom we have never seen, but, what is more, actually in an enemy, we need not be surprised if men's affections are roused when they fancy that they have seen virtue and goodness in those with whom a close intimacy is possible. I do not deny that affection is strengthened by the actual receipt of benefits, as well as by the perception of a wish to render service, combined with a closer intercourse. When these are added to the

original impulse of the heart, to which I have alluded, a quite surprising warmth of feeling springs up. And if any one thinks that this comes from a sense of weakness, that each may have some one to help him to his particular need, all I can say is that, when he maintains it to be born of want and poverty, he allows to friendship an origin very base, and a pedigree, if I may be allowed the expression, far from noble. If this had been the case, a man's inclination to friendship would be exactly in proportion to his low opinion of his own resources. Whereas the truth is quite the other way. For when a man's confidence in himself is greatest, when he is so fortified by virtue and wisdom as to want nothing and to feel absolutely self-dependent, it is then that he is most conspicuous for seeking out and keeping up friendships. Did Africanus, for example, want anything of me? Not the least in the world! Neither did I of him. In my case it was an admiration of his virtue, in his an opinion, maybe, which he entertained of my character, that caused our affection. Closer intimacy added to the warmth of our feelings. But though many great material advantages did ensue, they were not the source from which our affection proceeded. For as we are not beneficent and liberal with any view of extorting gratitude, and do not regard an act of kindness as an investment, but follow a natural inclination to liberality; so we look on friendship as worth trying for, not because we are attracted to it by the expectation of ulterior gain, but in the conviction that what it has to give us is from first to last included in the feeling itself.

Far different is the view of those who, like brute beasts, refer everything to sensual pleasure. And no wonder. Men who have degraded all their powers of thought to an object so mean and contemptible can of course raise their eyes to nothing lofty, to nothing grand and divine. Such persons indeed let us leave out of the present question. And let us accept the doctrine that the sensation of love and the warmth of inclination have their origin in a spontaneous feeling which arises directly the presence of probity is indicated. When once men have conceived the inclination, they of course try to attach themselves to the object of it, and move themselves nearer and nearer to him. Their aim is that they may be on the same footing and the same level in regard to affection, and be more inclined to do a good service than to ask a return, and that there should be this noble rivalry between them. Thus both truths will be established. We shall get the most important material advantages from friendship; and its origin from a natural impulse rather than from a sense of need will be at once more dignified and more in accordance with fact. For if it were true that its material advantages cemented friendship, it would be equally true that any change in them would dissolve it. But nature being incapable of change, it follows that genuine friendships are eternal.

So much for the origin of friendship. But perhaps you would not care to hear any more.

Fannius. Nay, pray go on; let us have the rest, Laelius. I take on myself to speak for my friend here as his senior.

Scaevola. Quite right! Therefore, pray let us hear.

10. *Loelius.* Well, then, my good friends, listen to some conversations about friendship which very frequently passed

between Scipio and myself. I must begin by telling you, however, that he used to say that the most difficult thing in the world was for a friendship to remain unimpaired to the end of life. So many things might intervene: conflicting interests; differences of opinion in politics; frequent changes in character, owing sometimes to misfortunes, sometimes to advancing years. He used to illustrate these facts from the analogy of boyhood, since the warmest affections between boys are often laid aside with the boyish toga; and even if they did manage to keep them up to adolescence, they were sometimes broken by a rivalry in courtship, or for some other advantage to which their mutual claims were not compatible. Even if the friendship was prolonged beyond that time, yet it frequently received a rude shock should the two happen to be competitors for office. For while the most fatal blow to friendship in the majority of cases was the lust of gold, in the case of the best men it was a rivalry for office and reputation, by which it had often happened that the most violent enmity had arisen between the closest friends.

Again, wide breaches and, for the most part, justifiable ones were caused by an immoral request being made of friends, to pander to a man's unholy desires or to assist him in inflicting a wrong. A refusal, though perfectly right, is attacked by those to whom they refuse compliance as a violation of the laws of friendship. Now the people who have no scruples as to the requests they make to their friends, thereby allow that they are ready to have no scruples as to what they will do *for* their friends; and it is the recriminations of such people which commonly not only quench friendships, but give rise to lasting enmities. 'In fact,' he used to say, 'these fatalities overhang friendship in such numbers that it requires not only wisdom but good luck also to escape them all.'

11. With these premises, then, let us first, if you please, examine the question – how far ought personal feeling to go in friendship? For instance: suppose Coriolanus to have had friends, ought they to have joined him in invading his country? Again, in the case of Vecellinus or Spurius Maelius, ought their friends to have assisted them in their attempt to establish a tyranny? Take two instances of either line of conduct. When Tiberius Gracchus attempted his revolutionary measures he was deserted, as we saw, by Quintus Tubero and the friends of his own standing. On the other hand, a friend of your own family, Scaevola, Gaius Blossius of Cumae, took a different course. I was acting as assessor to the consuls Laenas and Rupilius to try the conspirators, and Blossius pleaded for my pardon on the ground that his regard for Tiberius Gracchus had been so high that he looked upon his wishes as law. 'Even if he had wished you to set fire to the Capitol?' said I. 'That is a thing,' he replied, 'that he never would have wished.' 'Ah, but if he had wished it?' said I. 'I would have obeyed.' The wickedness of such a speech needs no comment. And in point of fact he was as good and better than his word for he did not wait for orders in the audacious proceedings of Tiberius Gracchus, but was the head and front of them, and was a leader rather than an abettor of his madness. The result of his infatuation was that he fled to Asia, terrified by the special commission appointed to try him, joined the enemies of his country, and paid a penalty to the republic

as heavy as it was deserved. I conclude, then, that the plea of having acted in the interests of a friend is not a valid excuse for a wrong action. For, seeing that a belief in a man's virtue is the original cause of friendship, friendship can hardly remain if virtue be abandoned. But if we decide it to be right to grant our friends whatever they wish, and to ask them for whatever we wish, perfect wisdom must be assumed on both sides if no mischief is to happen. But we cannot assume this perfect wisdom; for we are speaking only of such friends as are ordinarily to be met with, whether we have actually seen them or have been told about them – men, that is to say, of everyday life. I must quote some examples of such persons, taking care to select such as approach nearest to our standard of wisdom. We read, for instance, that Papus Aemilius was a close friend of Gaius Luscinus. History tells us that they were twice consuls together, and colleagues in the censorship. Again, it is on record that Manius Curius and Tiberius Coruncanius were on the most intimate terms with them and with each other. Now, we cannot even suspect that any one of these men ever asked of his friend anything that militated against his honour or his oath or the interests of the republic. In the case of such men as these there is no point in saying that one of them would not have obtained such a request if he had made it; for they were men of the most scrupulous piety, and the making of such a request would involve a breach of religious obligation no less than the granting it. However, it is quite true that Gaius Carbo and Gaius Cato did follow Tiberius Gracchus; and though his brother Caius Gracchus did not do so at the time, he is now the most eager of them all.

12. We may then lay down this rule of friendship – *neither ask nor consent to do what is wrong*. For the plea 'for friendship's sake' is a discreditable one, and not to be admitted for a moment. This rule holds good for all wrong-doing, but more especially in such as involves disloyalty to the republic. For things have come to such a point with us, my dear Fannius and Scaevola, that we are bound to look somewhat far ahead to what is likely to happen to the republic. The constitution, as known to our ancestors, has already swerved somewhat from the regular course and the lines marked out for it. Tiberius Gracchus made an attempt to obtain the power of a king, or, I might rather say, enjoyed that power for a few months. Had the Roman people ever heard or seen the like before? What the friends and connexions that followed him, even after his death, have succeeded in doing in the case of Publius Scipio I cannot describe without tears. As for Carbo, thanks to the punishment recently inflicted on Tiberius Gracchus, we have by hook or by crook managed to hold out against his attacks. But what to expect of the tribuneship of Caius Gracchus I do not like to forecast. One thing leads to another; and once set going, the downward course proceeds with ever-increasing velocity. There is the case of the ballot: what a blow was inflicted first by the lex Gabinia, and two years afterwards by the lex Cassia! I seem already to see the people estranged from the Senate, and the most important affairs at the mercy of the multitude. For you may be sure that more people will learn how to set such things in motion than how to stop them. What is the point of these remarks? This: no one ever makes any attempt of this sort without friends to help him. We must therefore

impress upon good men that, should they become inevitably involved in friendships with men of this kind, they ought not to consider themselves under any obligation to stand by friends who are disloyal to the republic. Bad men must have the fear of punishment before their eyes: a punishment not less severe for those who follow than for those who lead others to crime. Who was more famous and powerful in Greece than Themistocles? At the head of the army in the Persian war he had freed Greece; he owed his exile to personal envy: but he did not submit to the wrong done him by his ungrateful country as he ought to have done. He acted as Coriolanus had acted among us twenty years before. But no one was found to help them in their attacks upon their fatherland. Both of them accordingly committed suicide.

We conclude, then, not only that no such confederation of evilly disposed men must be allowed to shelter itself under the plea of friendship, but that, on the contrary, it must be visited with the severest punishment, lest the idea should prevail that fidelity to a friend justifies even making war upon one's country. And this is a case which I am inclined to think, considering how things are beginning to go, will sooner or later arise. And I care quite as much what the state of the constitution will be after my death as what it is now.

13. Let this, then, be laid down as the first law of friendship, that *we should ask from friends, and do for friends, only what is good*. But do not let us wait to be asked either: let there be ever an eager readiness, and an absence of hesitation. Let us have the courage to give advice with

candour. In friendship, let the influence of friends who give good advice be paramount; and let this influence be used to enforce advice not only in plain-spoken terms, but sometimes, if the case demands it, with sharpness; and when so used, let it be obeyed.

I give you these rules because I believe that some wonderful opinions are entertained by certain persons who have, I am told, a reputation for wisdom in Greece. There is nothing in the world, by the way, beyond the reach of their sophistry. Well, some of them teach that we should avoid very close friendships, for fear that one man should have to endure the anxieties of several. Each man, say they, has enough and to spare on his own hands; it is too bad to be involved in the cares of other people. The wisest course is to hold the reins of friendship as loose as possible; you can then tighten or slacken them at your will. For the first condition of a happy life is freedom from care, which no one's mind can enjoy if it has to travail, so to speak, for others besides itself. Another sect, I am told, gives vent to opinions still less generous. I briefly touched on this subject just now. They affirm that friendships should be sought solely for the sake of the assistance they give, and not at all from motives of feeling and affection; and that therefore just in proportion as a man's power and means of support are lowest, he is most eager to gain friendships: thence it comes that weak women seek the support of friendship more than men, the poor more than the rich, the unfortunate rather than those esteemed prosperous. What noble philosophy! You might just as well take the sun out of the sky as friendship from life; for the immortal gods have given us nothing better or more delightful.

But let us examine the two doctrines. What is the value of this 'freedom from care'? It is very tempting at first sight, but in practice it has in many cases to be put on one side. For there is no business and no course of action demanded from us by our honour which you can consistently decline, or lay aside when begun, from a mere wish to escape from anxiety. Nay, if we wish to avoid anxiety we must avoid virtue itself, which necessarily involves some anxious thoughts in showing its loathing and abhorrence for the qualities which are opposite to itself – as kindness for ill-nature, self-control for licentiousness, courage for cowardice. Thus you may notice that it is the just who are most pained at injustice, the brave at cowardly actions, the temperate at depravity. It is then characteristic of a rightly ordered mind to be pleased at what is good and grieved at the reverse. Seeing then that the wise are not exempt from the heart-ache (which must be the case unless we suppose all human nature rooted out of their hearts), why should we banish friendship from our lives, for fear of being involved by it in some amount of distress? If you take away emotion, what difference remains I don't say between a man and a beast, but between a man and a stone or a log of wood, or anything else of that kind?

Neither should we give any weight to the doctrine that virtue is something rigid and unyielding as iron. In point of fact it is in regard to friendship, as in so many other things, so supple and sensitive that it expands, so to speak, at a friend's good fortune, contracts at his misfortunes. We conclude then that mental pain which we must often encounter on a friend's account is not of sufficient consequence to banish friendship from our life, any more than it is true that the cardinal virtues are to be dispensed with because they involve certain anxieties and distresses.

14. Let me repeat then, 'the clear indication of virtue, to which a mind of like character is naturally attracted, is the beginning of friendship.' When that is the case the rise of affection is a necessity. For what can be more irrational than to take delight in many objects incapable of response, such as office, fame, splendid buildings, and personal decoration, and yet to take little or none in a sentient being endowed with virtue, which has the faculty of loving or, if I may use the expression, loving back? For nothing is really more delightful than a return of affection, and the mutual interchange of kind feeling and good offices. And if we add, as we may fairly do, that nothing so powerfully attracts and draws one thing to itself as likeness does to friendship, it will at once be admitted to be true that the good love the good and attach them to themselves as though they were united by blood and nature. For nothing can be more eager, or rather greedy, for what is like itself than nature. So, my dear Fannius and Scaevola, we may look upon this as an established fact, that between good men there is, as it were of necessity, a kindly feeling, which is the source of friendship ordained by nature. But this same kindliness affects the many also. For that is no unsympathetic or selfish or exclusive virtue, which protects even whole nations and consults their best interests. And that certainly it would not have done had it disdained all affection for the common herd.

Again, the believers in the 'interest' theory appear to me to destroy the most attractive link in the chain of friendship.

For it is not so much what one gets by a friend that gives one pleasure, as the warmth of his feeling; and we only care for a friend's service if it has been prompted by affection. And so far from its being true that lack of means is a motive for seeking friendship, it is usually those who, being most richly endowed with wealth and means, and above all with virtue (which, after all, is a man's best support), are least in need of another, that are most open-handed and beneficent. Indeed I am inclined to think that friends ought at times to be in want of something. For instance, what scope would my affections have had if Scipio had never wanted my advice or co-operation at home or abroad? It is not friendship, then, that follows material advantage, but material advantage friendship.

15. We must not therefore listen to these superfine gentlemen when they talk of friendship, which they know neither in theory nor in practice. For who, in heaven's name, would choose a life of the greatest wealth and abundance on condition of neither loving or being beloved by any creature? That is the sort of life tyrants endure. They, of course, can count on no fidelity, no affection, no security for the goodwill of any one. For them all is suspicion and anxiety; for them there is no possibility of friendship. Who can love one whom he fears, or by whom he knows that he is feared? Yet such men have a show of friendship offered them, but it is only a fair-weather show. If it ever happen that they fall, as it generally does, they will at once understand how friendless they are. So they say Tarquin observed in his exile that he never knew which of his friends were real and which sham, until he had ceased to be able

to repay either. Though what surprises me is that a man of his proud and overbearing character should have a friend at all. And as it was his character that prevented his having genuine friends, so it often happens in the case of men of unusually great means – their very wealth forbids faithful friendships. For not only is Fortune blind herself; but she generally makes those blind also who enjoy her favours. They are carried, so to speak, beyond themselves with self-conceit and self-will; nor can anything be more perfectly intolerable than a successful fool. You may often see it. Men who before had pleasant manners enough undergo a complete change on attaining power of office. They despise their old friends: devote themselves to new.

Now, can anything be more foolish than that men who have all the opportunities which prosperity, wealth, and great means can bestow, should secure all else which money can buy – horses, servants, splendid upholstering, and costly plate – but do not secure friends, who are, if I may use the expression, the most valuable and beautiful furniture of life? And yet, when they acquire the former, they know not who will enjoy them, nor for whom they may be taking all this trouble; for they will one and all eventually belong to the strongest: while each man has a stable and inalienable ownership in his friendships. And even if those possessions, which are, in a manner, the gifts of fortune, do prove permanent, life can never be anything but joyless which is without the consolations and companionship of friends.

16. To turn to another branch of our subject. We must now endeavour to ascertain what limits are to be observed in friendship – what is the boundary-line, so to speak, beyond

which our affection is not to go. On this point I notice three opinions, with none of which I agree. One is *that we should love our friend just as much as we love ourselves, and no more; another, that our affection to them should exactly correspond and equal theirs to us; a third, that a man should be valued at exactly the same rate as he values himself.* To not one of these opinions do I assent. The first, which holds that our regard for ourselves is to be the measure of our regard for our friend, is not true; for how many things there are which we would never have done for our own sakes, but do for the sake of a friend! We submit to make requests from unworthy people, to descend even to supplication; to be sharper in invective, more violent in attack. Such actions are not creditable in our own interests, but highly so in those of our friends. There are many advantages too which men of upright character voluntarily forgo, or of which they are content to be deprived, that their friends may enjoy them rather than themselves.

The second doctrine is that which limits friendship to an exact equality in mutual good offices and good feelings. But such a view reduces friendship to a question of figures in a spirit far too narrow and illiberal, as though the object were to have an exact balance in a debtor and creditor account. True friendship appears to me to be something richer and more generous than that comes to; and not to be so narrowly on its guard against giving more than it receives. In such a matter we must not be always afraid of something being wasted or running over in our measure, or of more than is justly due being devoted to our friendship.

But the last limit proposed is the worst, namely, that a friend's estimate of himself is to be the measure of our estimate of him. It often happens that a man has too humble an idea of himself, or takes too despairing a view of his chance of bettering his fortune. In such a case a friend ought not to take the view of him which he takes of himself. Rather he should do all he can to raise his drooping spirits, and lead him to more cheerful hopes and thoughts.

We must then find some other limit. But I must first mention the sentiment which used to call forth Scipio's severest criticism. He often said that no one ever gave utterance to anything more diametrically opposed to the spirit of friendship than the author of the dictum, 'You should love your friend with the consciousness that you may one day hate him.' He could not be induced to believe that it was rightfully attributed to Bias, who was counted as one of the Seven Sages. It was the sentiment of some person with sinister motives or selfish ambition, or who regarded everything as it affected his own supremacy. How can a man be friends with another, if he thinks it possible that he may be his enemy? Why, it will follow that he must wish and desire his friend to commit as many mistakes as possible, that he may have all the more handles against him; and, conversely, that he must be annoyed, irritated, and jealous at the right actions or good fortune of his friends. This maxim, then, let it be whose it will, is the utter destruction of friendship. The true rule is to take such care in the selection of our friends as never to enter upon a friendship with a man whom we could under any circumstances come to hate. And even if we are unlucky in our choice, we must put up with it – according to Scipio – in preference to making calculations as to a future breach.

17. The real limit to be observed in friendship is this: the characters of two friends must be stainless. There must be complete harmony of interests, purpose, and aims, without exception. Then if the case arises of a friend's wish (not strictly right in itself) calling for support in a matter involving his life or reputation, we must make some concession from the straight path – on condition, that is to say, that extreme disgrace is not the consequence. Something must be conceded to friendship. And yet we must not be entirely careless of our reputation, nor regard the good opinion of our fellow-citizens as a weapon which we can afford to despise in conducting the business of our life, however lowering it may be to tout for it by flattery and smooth words. We must by no means abjure virtue, which secures us affection.

But to return again to Scipio, the sole author of the discourse on friendship. He used to complain that there was nothing on which men bestowed so little pains: that every one could tell exactly how many goats or sheep he had, but not how many friends; and while they took pains in procuring the former, they were utterly careless in selecting friends, and possessed no particular marks, so to speak, or tokens by which they might judge of their suitability for friendship. Now the qualities we ought to look out for in making our selection are firmness, stability, constancy. There is a plentiful lack of men so endowed, and it is difficult to form a judgment without testing. Now this testing can only be made during the actual existence of the friendship; for friendship so often precedes the formation of a judgment, and makes a previous test impossible. If we are prudent then, we shall rein in our impulse to affection as we do chariot horses. We make a preliminary trial of horses. So we should of friendship; and should test our friends' characters by a kind of tentative friendship. It may often happen that the untrustworthiness of certain men is completely displayed in a small money matter; others who are proof against a small sum are detected if it be large. But even if some *are* found who think it mean to prefer money to friendship, where shall we look for those who put friendship before office, civil or military promotions, and political power, and who, when the choice lies between these things on the one side and the claims of friendship on the other, do not give a strong preference to the former? It is not in human nature to be indifferent to political power; and if the price men have to pay for it is the sacrifice of friendship, they think their treason will be thrown into the shade by the magnitude of the reward. This is why true friendship is very difficult to find among those who engage in politics and the contest for office. Where can you find the man to prefer his friend's advancement to his own? And to say nothing of that, think how grievous and almost intolerable it is to most men to share political disaster. You will scarcely find anyone who can bring himself to do that. And though what Ennius says is quite true – 'the hour of need shews the friend indeed,' – yet it is in these two ways that most people betray their untrustworthiness and inconstancy, by looking down on friends when they are themselves prosperous, or deserting them in their distress. A man, then, who has shewn a firm, unshaken, and unvarying friendship in both these contingencies we must reckon as one of a class the rarest in the world, and all but superhuman.

18. Now, what is the quality to look out for as a warrant for the stability and permanence of friendship? It is loyalty. Nothing that lacks this can be stable. We should also in making our selection look out for simplicity, a social disposition, and a sympathetic nature, moved by what moves us. These all contribute to maintain loyalty. You can never trust a character which is intricate and tortuous. Nor, indeed, is it possible for one to be trustworthy and firm who is unsympathetic by nature and unmoved by what affects ourselves. We may add, that he must neither take pleasure in bringing accusations against us himself, nor believe them when they are brought. All these contribute to form that constancy which I have been endeavouring to describe. And the result is, what I started by saying, that friendship is only possible between good men.

Now there are two characteristic features in his treatment of his friends that a good (which may be regarded as equivalent to a wise) man will always display. First, he will be entirely without any make-believe or pretence of feeling; for the open display even of dislike is more becoming to an ingenuous character than a studied concealment of sentiment. Secondly, he will not only reject all accusations brought against his friend by another, but he will not be suspicious himself either, nor be always thinking that his friend has acted improperly. Besides this, there should be a certain pleasantness in word and manner which adds no little flavour to friendship. A gloomy temper and unvarying gravity may be very impressive; but friendship should be a little less unbending, more indulgent and gracious, and more inclined to all kinds of good-fellowship and good-nature.

19. But here arises a question of some little difficulty. Are there any occasions on which, assuming their worthiness, we should prefer new to old friends, just as we prefer young to aged horses? The answer admits of no doubt whatever. For there should be no satiety in friendship, as there is in other things. The older the sweeter, as in wines that keep well. And the proverb is a true one, 'You must eat many a peck of salt with a man to be thorough friends with him.' Novelty, indeed, has its advantage, which we must not despise. There is always hope of fruit, as there is in healthy blades of corn. But age too must have its proper position; and, in fact, the influence of time and habit is very great. To recur to the illustration of the horse which I have just now used: every one likes *ceteris paribus* to use the horse to which he has been accustomed, rather than one that is untried and new. And it is not only in the case of a living thing that this rule holds good, but in inanimate things also; for we like places where we have lived the longest, even though they are mountainous and covered with forest. But here is another golden rule in friendship: *put yourself on a level with your friend*. For it often happens that there are certain superiorities, as for example Scipio's in what I may call our set. Now he never assumed any airs of superiority over Philus, or Rupilius, or Mummius, or over friends of a lower rank still. For instance, he always shewed a deference to his brother Quintus Maximus because he was his senior, who, though a man no doubt of eminent character, was by no means his equal. He used also to wish that all his friends should be the better for his support. This is an example we should all follow. If any of us have any advantage in personal character, intellect, or fortune, we

should be ready to make our friends sharers and partners in it with ourselves. For instance, if their parents are in humble circumstances, if their relations are powerful neither in intellect nor means, we should supply their deficiencies and promote their rank and dignity. You know the legends of children brought up as servants in ignorance of their parentage and family. When they are recognized and discovered to be the sons of gods or kings, they still retain their affection for the shepherds whom they have for many years looked upon as their parents. Much more ought this to be so in the case of real and undoubted parents. For the advantages of genius and virtue, and in short, of every kind of superiority, are never realized to their fullest extent until they are bestowed upon our nearest and dearest.

20. But the converse must also be observed. For in friendship and relationship, just as those who possess any superiority must put themselves on an equal footing with those who are less fortunate, so these latter must not be annoyed at being surpassed in genius, fortune, or rank. But most people of that sort are forever either grumbling at something, or harping on their claims; and especially if they consider that they have services of their own to allege involving zeal and friendship and some trouble to themselves. People who are always bringing up their services are a nuisance. The recipient ought to remember them; the performer should never mention them. In the case of friends, then, as the superior are bound to descend, so are they bound in a certain sense to raise those below them. For there are people who make their friendship disagreeable by imagining themselves undervalued. This generally happens only to

those who think that they deserve to be so; and they ought to be shewn by deeds as well as by words the groundlessness of their opinion. Now the measure of your benefits should be in the first place your own power to bestow, and in the second place the capacity to bear them on the part of him on whom you are bestowing affection and help. For, however great your personal prestige may be, you cannot raise all your friends to the highest offices of the State. For instance, Scipio was able to make Publius Rupilius consul, but not his brother Lucius. But granting that you can give anyone anything you choose, you must have a care that it does not prove to be beyond his powers. As a general rule, we must wait to make up our mind about friendships till men's characters and years have arrived at their full strength and development. People must not, for instance, regard as fast friends all whom in their youthful enthusiasm for hunting or football they liked for having the same tastes. By that rule, if it were a mere question of time, no one would have such claims on our affections as nurses and slave-tutors. Not that they are to be neglected, but they stand on a different ground. It is only these mature friendships that can be permanent. For difference of character leads to difference of aims, and the result of such diversity is to estrange friends. The sole reason, for instance, which prevents good men from making friends with bad, or bad with good, is that the divergence of their characters and aims is the greatest possible.

Another good rule in friendship is this: do not let an excessive affection hinder the highest interests of your friends. This very often happens. I will go again to the region of fable for an instance. Neoptolemus could never have taken Troy if he had been willing to listen to Lycomedes, who had brought him up, and with many tears tried to prevent his going there. Again, it often happens that important business makes it necessary to part from friends: the man who tries to baulk it, because he thinks that he cannot endure the separation, is of a weak and effeminate nature, and on that very account makes but a poor friend. There are, of course, limits to what you ought to expect from a friend and to what you should allow him to demand of you. And these you must take into calculation in every case.

21. Again, there is such a disaster, so to speak, as having to break off friendship. And sometimes it is one we cannot avoid. For at this point the stream of our discourse is leaving the intimacies of the wise and touching on the friendship of ordinary people. It will happen at times that an outbreak of vicious conduct affects either a man's friends themselves or strangers, yet the discredit falls on the friends. In such cases friendships should be allowed to die out gradually by an intermission of intercourse. They should, as I have been told that Cato used to say, rather be unstitched than torn in twain; unless, indeed, the injurious conduct be of so violent and outrageous a nature as to make an instant breach and separation the only possible course consistent with honour and rectitude. Again, if a change in character and aim takes place, as often happens, or if party politics produces an alienation of feeling (I am now speaking, as I said a short time ago, of ordinary friendships, not of those of the wise), we shall have to be on our guard against appearing to embark upon active enmity while we only

mean to resign a friendship. For there can be nothing more discreditable than to be at open war with a man with whom you have been intimate. Scipio, as you are aware, had abandoned his friendship for Quintus Pompeius on my account; and again, from differences of opinion in politics, he became estranged from my colleague Metellus. In both cases he acted with dignity and moderation, shewing that he was offended indeed, but without rancour.

Our first object, then, should be to prevent a breach; our second, to secure that, if it does occur, our friendship should seem to have died a natural rather than a violent death. Next, we should take care that friendship is not converted into active hostility, from which flow personal quarrels, abusive language, and angry recriminations. These last, however, provided that they do not pass all reasonable limits of forbearance, we ought to put up with, and, in compliment to an old friendship, allow the party that inflicts the injury, not the one that submits to it, to be in the wrong. Generally speaking, there is but one way of securing and providing oneself against faults and inconveniences of this sort – not to be too hasty in bestowing our affection, and not to bestow it at all on unworthy objects.

Now, by 'worthy of friendship' I mean those who have in themselves the qualities which attract affection. This sort of man is rare; and indeed all excellent things are rare; and nothing in the world is so hard to find as a thing entirely and completely perfect of its kind. But most people not only recognize nothing as good in our life unless it is profitable, but look upon friends as so much stock, caring most for those by whom they hope to make most profit. Accordingly they never possess that most beautiful and most spontaneous friendship which must be sought solely for itself without any ulterior object. They fail also to learn from their own feelings the nature and the strength of friendship. For every one loves himself, not for any reward which such love may bring, but because he is dear to himself independently of anything else. But unless this feeling is transferred to another, what a real friend is will never be revealed; for he is, as it were, a second self. But if we find these two instincts shewing themselves in animals – whether of the air or the sea or the land, whether wild or tame – first, a love of self, which in fact is born in everything that lives alike; and, secondly, an eagerness to find and attach themselves to other creatures of their own kind; and if this natural action is accompanied by desire and by something resembling human love, how much more must this be the case in man by the law of his nature? For man not only loves himself, but seeks another whose spirit he may so blend with his own as almost to make one being of two.

22. But most people unreasonably, not to speak of modesty, want such a friend as they are unable to be themselves, and expect from their friends what they do not themselves give. The fair course is first to be good yourself, and then to look out for another of like character. It is between such that the stability in friendship of which we have been talking can be secured; when, that is to say, men who are united by affection learn, first of all, to rule those passions which enslave others, and in the next place to take delight in fair and equitable conduct, to bear each other's burdens, never to ask each other for anything inconsistent with virtue and rectitude, and not only to serve and love but also to respect

each other. I say 'respect'; for if respect is gone, friendship has lost its brightest jewel. And this shows the mistake of those who imagine that friendship gives a privilege to licentiousness and sin. Nature has given us friendship as the handmaid of virtue, not as a partner in guilt: to the end that virtue, being powerless when isolated to reach the highest objects, might succeed in doing so in union and partnership with another. Those who enjoy in the present, or have enjoyed in the past, or are destined to enjoy in the future such a partnership as this, must be considered to have secured the most excellent and auspicious combination for reaching nature's highest good. This is the partnership, I say, which combines moral rectitude, fame, peace of mind, serenity: all that men think desirable because with them life is happy, but without them cannot be so. This being our best and highest object, we must, if we desire to attain it, devote ourselves to virtue; for without virtue we can obtain neither friendship nor anything else desirable. In fact, if virtue be neglected, those who imagine themselves to possess friends will find out their error as soon as some grave disaster forces them to make trial of them. Wherefore, I must again and again repeat, you must satisfy your judgment before engaging your affections: not love first and judge afterwards. We suffer from carelessness in many of our undertakings: in none more than in selecting and cultivating our friends. We put the cart before the horse, and shut the stable door when the steed is stolen, in defiance of the old proverb. For, having mutually involved ourselves in a long-standing intimacy or by actual obligations, all on a sudden some cause of offence arises and we break off our friendships in full career.

23. It is this that makes such carelessness in a matter of supreme importance all the more worthy of blame. I say 'supreme importance', because friendship is the one thing about the utility of which everybody with one accord is agreed. That is not the case in regard even to virtue itself; for many people speak slightingly of virtue as though it were mere puffing and self-glorification. Nor is it the case with riches. Many look down on riches, being content with a little and taking pleasure in poor fare and dress. And as to the political offices for which some have a burning desire – how many entertain such a contempt for them as to think nothing in the world more empty and trivial!

And so on with the rest; things desirable in the eyes of some are regarded by very many as worthless. But of friendship all think alike to a man, whether those have devoted themselves to politics, or those who delight in science and philosophy, or those who follow a private way of life and care for nothing but their own business, or those lastly who have given themselves body and soul to sensuality – they all think, I say, that without friendship life is no life, if they want some part of it, at any rate, to be noble. For friendship, in one way or another, penetrates into the lives of us all, and suffers no career to be entirely free from its influence. Though a man be of so churlish and unsociable a nature as to loathe and shun the company of mankind, as we are told was the case with a certain Timon at Athens, yet even he cannot refrain from seeking some one in whose hearing he may disgorge the venom of his bitter temper. We should see this most clearly, if it were possible that some god should carry us away from these haunts of men, and place us somewhere in perfect solitude, and then should supply us in abundance with everything necessary to our nature, and yet take from us entirely the opportunity of looking upon a human being. Who could steel himself to endure such a life? Who would not lose in his loneliness the zest for all pleasures? And indeed this is the point of the observation of, I think, Archytas of Tarentum. I have it third hand; men who were my seniors told me that their seniors had told them. It was this: 'If a man could ascend to heaven and get a clear view of the natural order of the universe, and the beauty of the heavenly bodies, that wonderful spectacle would give him small pleasure, though nothing could be conceived more delightful if he had but had some one to whom to tell what he had seen.' So true it is that nature abhors isolation, and ever leans upon something as a stay and support; and this is found in its most pleasing form in our closest friend.

24. But though Nature also declares by so many indications what her wish and object and desire is, we yet in a manner turn a deaf ear and will not hear her warnings. The intercourse between friends is varied and complex, and it must often happen that causes of suspicion and offence arise, which a wise man will sometimes avoid, at other times remove, at others treat with indulgence. The one possible cause of offence that must be faced is when the interests of your friend and your own sincerity are at stake. For instance, it often happens that friends need remonstrance and even reproof. When these are administered in a kindly spirit they ought to be taken in good part. But somehow or other there is truth in what my friend Terence says in his *Andria*:

Compliance gets us friends, plain speaking hate.

Plain speaking is a cause of trouble, if the result of it is resentment, which is poison of friendship; but compliance is really the cause of much more trouble, because by indulging his faults it lets a friend plunge into headlong ruin. But the man who is most to blame is he who resents plain speaking and allows flattery to egg him on to his ruin. On this point, then, from first to last there is need of deliberation and care. If we remonstrate, it should be without bitterness; if we reprove, there should be no word of insult. In the matter of compliance (for I am glad to adopt Terence's word), though there should be every courtesy, yet that base kind which assists a man in vice should be far from us, for it is unworthy of a free-born man, to say nothing of a friend. It is one thing to live with a tyrant, another with a friend. But if a man's ears are so closed to plain speaking that he cannot bear to hear the truth from a friend, we may give him up in despair. This remark of Cato's, as so many of his did, shews great acuteness: 'There are people who owe more to bitter enemies than to apparently pleasant friends: the former often speak the truth, the latter never.' Besides, it is a strange paradox that the recipients of advice should feel no annoyance where they ought to feel it, and yet feel so much where they ought not. They are not at all vexed at having committed a fault, but very angry at being reproved for it. On the contrary, they ought to be grieved at the crime and glad of the correction.

25. Well, then, if it is true that to give and receive advice – the former with freedom and yet without bitterness, the latter with patience and without irritation – is peculiarly

appropriate to genuine friendship, it is no less true that there can be nothing more utterly subversive of friendship than flattery, adulation, and base compliance. I use as many terms as possible to brand this vice of light-minded, untrustworthy men, whose sole object in speaking is to please without any regard to truth. In everything false pretence is bad, for it suspends and vitiates our power of discerning the truth. But to nothing is it so hostile as to friendship; for it destroys that frankness without which friendship is an empty name. For the essence of friendship being that two minds become as one, how can that ever take place if the mind of each of the separate parties to it is not single and uniform, but variable, changeable, and complex? Can anything be so pliable, so wavering, as the mind of a man whose attitude depends not only on another's feeling and wish, but on his very looks and nods?

> *If one says 'No,' I answer 'No'; if 'Yes,' I answer*
> *'Yes.'*
> *In fine, I've laid this task upon myself*
> *To echo all that's said—*

to quote my old friend Terence again. But he puts these words into the mouth of a Gnatho. To admit such a man into one's intimacy at all is a sign of folly. But there are many people like Gnatho, and it is when they are superior either in position or fortune or reputation that their flatteries become mischievous, the weight of their position making up for the lightness of their character. But if we only take reasonable care, it is as easy to separate and distinguish a genuine from a specious friend as anything else that is coloured and artificial from what is sincere and genuine. A public assembly, though composed of men of the smallest possible culture, nevertheless will see clearly the difference between a mere demagogue (that is, a flatterer and untrustworthy citizen) and a man of principle, standing, and solidity. It was by this kind of flattering language that Gaius Papirius the other day endeavoured to tickle the ears of the assembled people, when proposing his law to make the tribunes re-eligible. I spoke against it. But I will leave the personal question. I prefer speaking of Scipio. Good heavens! How impressive his speech was, what a majesty there was in it! You would have pronounced him, without hesitation, to be no mere henchman of the Roman people, but their leader. However, you were there, and moreover have the speech in your hands. The result was that a law meant to please the people was by the people's votes rejected. Once more to refer to myself, you remember how apparently popular was the law proposed by Gaius Licinius Crassus 'about the election to the College of Priests' in the consulship of Quintus Maximus, Scipio's brother, and Lucius Mancinus. For the power of filling up their own vacancies on the part of the colleges was by this proposal to be transferred to the people. It was this man, by the way, who began the practice of turning towards the forum when addressing the people. In spite of this, however, upon my speaking on the conservative side, religion gained an easy victory over his plausible speech. This took place in my praetorship, five years before I was elected consul, which shows that the cause was successfully maintained more by the merits of the case than by the prestige of the highest office.

26. Now, if on a stage, such as a public assembly essentially

is, where there is the amplest room for fiction and half-truths, truth nevertheless prevails if it be but fairly laid open and brought into the light of day, what ought to happen in the case of friendship, which rests entirely on truthfulness? Friendship, in which, unless you both see and show an open breast, to use a common expression, you can neither trust nor be certain of anything—no, not even of mutual affection, since you cannot be sure of its sincerity. However, this flattery, injurious as it is, can hurt no one but the man who takes it in and likes it. And it follows that the man to open his ears widest to flatterers is he who first flatters himself and is fondest of himself. I grant you that Virtue naturally loves herself; for she knows herself and perceives how worthy of love she is. But I am not now speaking of absolute virtue, but of the belief men have that they possess virtue. The fact is that fewer people are endowed with virtue than wish to be thought to be so. It is such people that take delight in flattery. When they are addressed in language expressly adapted to flatter their vanity, they look upon such empty persiflage as a testimony to the truth of their own praises. It is not then properly friendship at all when the one will not listen to the truth, and the other is prepared to lie. Nor would the servility of parasites in comedy have seemed humorous to us had there been no such things as braggart captains. 'Is Thais really much obliged to me?' It would have been quite enough to answer 'Much', but he must needs say 'Immensely'. Your servile flatterer always exaggerates what his victim wishes to be put strongly. Wherefore, though it is with those who catch at and invite it that this flattering falsehood is especially powerful, yet men even of solider and steadier character must be warned to be on the watch against being taken in by cunningly disguised flattery. An open flatterer any one can detect, unless he is an absolute fool; the covert insinuation of the cunning and the sly is what we have to be studiously on our guard against. His detection is not by any means the easiest thing in the world, for he often covers his servility under the guise of contradiction, and flatters by pretending to dispute, and then at last giving in and allowing himself to be beaten, that the person hoodwinked may think himself to have been the clearer-sighted. Now what can be more degrading than to be thus hoodwinked? You must be on your guard against this happening to you, like the man in the *Heiress*:

> *How have I been befooled! no drivelling dotards*
> *On any stage were e'er so played upon.*

For even on the stage we have no grosser representation of folly than that of short-sighted and credulous old men. But somehow or other I have strayed away from the friendship of the perfect, that is of the 'wise' (meaning, of course, such 'wisdom' as human nature is capable of), to the subject of vulgar, unsubstantial friendships. Let us then return to our original theme, and at length bring that, too, to a conclusion.

27. Well, then, Fannius and Mucius, I repeat what I said before. It is virtue, virtue, which both creates and preserves friendship. On it depends harmony of interest, permanence, fidelity. When Virtue has reared her head and shewn the light of her countenance, and seen and recognized the same

light in another, she gravitates towards it, and in her turn welcomes that which the other has to shew; and from it springs up a flame which you may call love or friendship as you please. Both words are from the same root in Latin; and love is just the cleaving to him whom you love without the prompting of need or any view to advantage – though this latter blossoms spontaneously on friendship, little as you may have looked for it. It is with such warmth of feeling that I cherished Lucius Paulus, Marcus Cato, Gaius Gallus, Publius Nasica, Tiberius Gracchus, my dear Scipio's father-in-law. It shines with even greater warmth when men are of the same age, as in the case of Scipio and Lucius Furius, Publius Rupilius, Spurius Mummius, and myself. *En revanche*, in my old age I find comfort in the affection of young men, as in the case of yourselves and Quintus Tubero: nay more, I delight in the intimacy of such a very young man as Publius Rutilius and Aulus Verginius. And since the law of our nature and of our life is that a new generation is for ever springing up, the most desirable thing is that along with your contemporaries, with whom you started in the race, you may also reach what is to us the goal. But in view of the instability and perishableness of mortal things, we should be continually on the look-out for some to love and by whom to be loved; for if we lose affection and kindliness from our life, we lose all that gives it charm. For me, indeed, though torn away by a sudden stroke, Scipio still lives and ever will live. For it was the virtue of the man that I loved, and that has not suffered death. And it is not my eyes only, because I had all my life a personal experience of it, that never lose sight of it: it will shine to posterity also with undimmed glory. No one will ever cherish a nobler ambition or a loftier hope without thinking his memory and his image the best to put before his eyes. I declare that of all the blessings which either fortune or nature has bestowed upon me I know none to compare with Scipio's friendship. In it I found sympathy in public, counsel in private business; in it too a means of spending my leisure with unalloyed delight. Never, to the best of my knowledge, did I offend him even in the most trivial point; never did I hear a word from him I could have wished unsaid. We had one house, one table, one style of living; and not only were we together on foreign service, but in our tours also and country sojourns. Why speak of our eagerness to be ever gaining some knowledge, to be ever learning something, on which we spent all our leisure hours far from the gaze of the world? If the recollection and memory of these things had perished with the man, I could not possibly have endured the regret for one so closely united with me in life and affection. But these things have not perished; they are rather fed and strengthened by reflexion and memory. Even supposing me to have been entirely bereft of them, still my time of life of itself brings me no small consolation: for I cannot have much longer now to bear this regret; and everything that is brief ought to be endurable, however severe.

This is all I had to say on friendship. One piece of advice on parting. Make up your minds to this: virtue (without which friendship is impossible) is first; but next to it, and to it alone, the greatest of all things is Friendship.

ON OLD AGE

1. And should my service, Titus, ease the weight
Of care that wrings your heart, and draw the sting
Which rankles there, what guerdon shall there be?

FOR I may address you, Atticus, in the lines in which
Flamininus was addressed by the man,

who, poor in wealth, was rich in honour's gold,

though I am well assured that you are not, as Flamininus
was,

kept on the rack of care by night and day.

For I know how well ordered and equable your mind is,
and am fully aware that it was not a surname alone which
you brought home with you from Athens, but its culture
and good sense. And yet I have an idea that you are at
times stirred to the heart by the same circumstances as
myself. To console you for these is a more serious matter,
and must be put off to another time. For the present I have

resolved to dedicate to you an essay on Old Age. For from the burden of impending or at least advancing age, common to us both, I would do something to relieve us both though as to yourself I am fully aware that you support and will support it, as you do everything else, with calmness and philosophy. But directly I resolved to write on old age, you at once occurred to me as deserving a gift of which both of us might take advantage. To myself, indeed, the composition of this book has been so delightful that it has not only wiped away all the disagreeables of old age, but has even made it luxurious and delightful too. Never, therefore, can philosophy be praised as highly as it deserves considering that its faithful disciple is able to spend every period of his life with unruffled feelings. However, on other subjects I have spoken at large, and shall often speak again: this book which I herewith send you is on Old Age. I have put the whole discourse not, as Alisto of Cos did, in the mouth of Tithonus – for a mere fable would have lacked conviction – but in that of Marcus Cato when he was an old man, to give my essay greater weight. I represent Laelius and Scipio at his house expressing surprise at his carrying his years so lightly, and Cato answering them. If he shall seem to shew somewhat more learning in this discourse than he generally did in his own books, put it down to the Greek literature of which it is known that he became an eager student in his old age. But what need of more? Cato's own words will at once explain all I feel about old age.

M. Cato. Publius Cornelius Scipio Africanus (the younger). Gaius Laelius.

2. *Scipio*. Many a time have I in conversation with my friend Gaius Laelius here expressed my admiration, Marcus Cato, of the eminent, nay perfect, wisdom displayed by you indeed at all points, but above everything because I have noticed that old age never seemed a burden to you, while to most old men it is so hateful that they declare themselves under a weight heavier than Aetna.

Cato. Your admiration is easily excited, it seems, my dear Scipio and Laelius. Men, of course, who have no resources in themselves for securing a good and happy life find every age burdensome. But those who look for all happiness from within can never think anything bad which nature makes inevitable. In that category before anything else comes old age, to which all wish to attain, and at which all grumble when attained. Such is Folly's inconsistency and unreasonableness! They say that it is stealing upon them faster than they expected. In the first place, who compelled them to hug an illusion? For in what respect did old age steal upon manhood faster than manhood upon childhood? In the next place, in what way would old age have been less disagreeable to them if they were in their eight-hundredth year than in their eightieth? For their past, however long, when once it was past, would have no consolation for a stupid old age. Wherefore, if it is your wont to admire my wisdom – and I would that it were worthy of your good opinion and of my own surname of Sapiens – it really consists in the fact that I follow Nature, the best of guides, as I would a god, and am loyal to her commands. It is not likely, if she has written the rest of the play well, that she has been careless about the last act like some idle poet. But after all some 'last' was inevitable, just as to the berries of a tree and the fruits of the earth there comes in the fulness of time a period of decay and fall. A wise man will not make a grievance of this. To rebel against nature – is not that to fight like the giants with the gods?

Laelius. And yet, Cato, you will do us a very great favour (I venture to speak for Scipio as for myself) if – since we all hope, or at least wish, to become old men – you would allow us to learn from you in good time before it arrives, by what methods we may most easily acquire the strength to support the burden of advancing age.

Cato. I will do so without doubt, Laelius, especially if, as you say, it will be agreeable to you both.

Laelius. We do wish very much, Cato, if it is no trouble to you, to be allowed to see the nature of the bourne which you have reached after completing a long journey, as it were, upon which we too are bound to embark.

3. *Cato.* I will do the best I can, Laelius. It has often been my fortune to bear the complaints of my contemporaries – like will to like, you know, according to the old proverb – complaints to which men like C. Salinator and Sp. Albinus, who were of consular rank and about my time, used to give vent. They were, first, that they had lost the pleasures of the senses, without which they did not regard life as life at all; and, secondly, that they were neglected by those from whom they had been used to receive attentions. Such men appear to me to lay the blame on the wrong thing. For if

it had been the fault of old age, then these same misfortunes would have befallen me and all other men of advanced years. But I have known many of them who never said a word of complaint against old age; for they were only too glad to be freed from the bondage of passion, and were not at all looked down upon by their friends. The fact is that the blame for all complaints of that kind is to be charged to character, not to a particular time of life. For old men who are reasonable and neither cross-grained nor churlish find old age tolerable enough: whereas unreason and churlishness cause uneasiness at every time of life.

Laelius. It is as you say, Cato. But perhaps some one may suggest that it is your large means, wealth, and high position that make you think old age tolerable: whereas such good fortune only falls to few.

Cato. There is something in that, Laelius, but by no means all. For instance, the story is told of the answer of Themistocles in a wrangle with a certain Seriphian, who asserted that he owed his brilliant position to the reputation of his country, not to his own. 'If I had been a Seriphian,' said he, 'even I should never have been famous, nor would you if you had been an Athenian.' Something like this may be said of old age. For the philosopher himself could not find old age easy to bear in the depths of poverty, nor the fool feel it anything but a burden though he were a millionaire. You may be sure, my dear Scipio and Laelius, that the arms best adapted to old age are culture and the active exercise of the virtues. For if they have been maintained at every period – if one has lived much as well as long – the harvest they produce is wonderful, not only because they never fail us even in our last days (though that in itself is supremely important), but also because the consciousness of a well-spent life and the recollection of many virtuous actions are exceedingly delightful.

4. Take the case of Q. Fabius Maximus, the man, I mean, who recovered Tarentum. When I was a young man and he an old one, I was as much attached to him as if he had been my contemporary. For that great man's serious dignity was tempered by courteous manners, nor had old age made any change in his character. True, he was not exactly an old man when my devotion to him began, yet he was nevertheless well on in life; for his first consulship fell in the year after my birth. When quite a stripling I went with him in his fourth consulship as a soldier in the ranks, on the expedition against Capua, and in the fifth year after that against Tarentum. Four years after that I was elected quaestor, holding office in the consulship of Tuditanus and Cethegus, in which year, indeed, he as a very old man spoke in favour of the Cincian law 'on gifts and fees'.

Now this man conducted wars with all the spirit of youth when he was far advanced in life, and by his persistence gradually wearied out Hannibal, when rioting in all the confidence of youth. How brilliant are those lines of my friend Ennius on him!

> *For us, down beaten by the storms of fate,*
> *One man by wise delays restored the State.*
> *Praise or dispraise moved not his constant mood,*
> *True to his purpose, to his country's good!*

Down ever-lengthening avenues of fame
Thus shines and shall shine still his glorious name.

Again what vigilance, what profound skill did he show in
the capture of Tarentum! It was indeed in my hearing that
he made the famous retort to Salinator, who had retreated
into the citadel after losing the town: 'It was owing to me,
Quintus Fabius, that you retook Tarentum.' 'Quite so,' he
replied with a laugh; 'for had you not lost it, I should never
have recovered it.' Nor was he less eminent in civil life than
in war. In his second consulship, though his colleague would
not move in the matter, he resisted as long as he could the
proposal of the tribune C. Flaminius to divide the territory
of the Picenians and Gauls in free allotments in defiance of
a resolution of the Senate. Again, though he was an augur,
he ventured to say that whatever was done in the interests
of the State was done with the best possible auspices, that
any laws proposed against its interest were proposed against
the auspices. I was cognisant of much that was admirable
in that great man, but nothing struck me with greater
astonishment than the way in which he bore the death of
his son – a man of brilliant character and who had been
consul. His funeral speech over him is in wide circulation,
and when we read it, is there any philosopher of whom we
do not think meanly? Nor in truth was he only great in the
light of day and in the sight of his fellow-citizens; he was
still more eminent in private and at home. What a wealth
of conversation! What weighty maxims! What a wide
acquaintance with ancient history! What an accurate
knowledge of the science of augury! For a Roman, too, he
had a great tincture of letters. He had a tenacious memory

for military history of every sort, whether of Roman or foreign wars. And I used at that time to enjoy his conversation with a passionate eagerness, as though I already divined, what actually turned out to be the case, that when he died there would be no one to teach me anything.

5. What then is the purpose of such a long disquisition on Maximus? It is because you now see that an old age like his cannot conscientiously be called unhappy. Yet it is after all true that everybody cannot be a Scipio or a Maximus, with stormings of cities, with battles by land and sea, with wars in which they themselves commanded, and with triumphs to recall. Besides this there is a quiet, pure, and cultivated life which produces a calm and gentle old age, such as we have been told Plato's was, who died at his writing-desk in his eighty-first year; or like that of Isocrates, who says that he wrote the book called *The Panegyric* in his ninety-fourth year, and who lived for five years afterwards; while his master Gorgias of Leontini completed a hundred and seven years without ever relaxing his diligence or giving up work. When some one asked him why he consented to remain so long alive – 'I have no fault', said he, 'to find with old age.' That was a noble answer, and worthy of a scholar. For fools impute their own frailties and guilt to old age, contrary to the practice of Ennui, whom I mentioned just now. In the lines –

> *Like some brave steed that oft before*
> *The Olympic wreath of victory bore,*
> *Now by the weight of years oppressed,*
> *Forgets the race, and takes his rest –*

he compares his own old age to that of a high-spirited and successful race-horse. And him indeed you may very well remember. For the present consuls Titus Flamininus and Manius Acilius were elected in the nineteenth year after his death; and his death occurred in the consulship of Caepio and Philippus, the latter consul for the second time: in which year I, then sixty-six years old, spoke in favour of the Voconian law in a voice that was still strong and with lungs still sound; while he, though seventy years old, supported two burdens considered the heaviest of all – poverty and old age – in such a way as to be all but fond of them.

The fact is that when I come to think it over, I find that there are four reasons for old age being thought unhappy: First, that it withdraws us from active employments; second, that it enfeebles the body; third, that it deprives us of nearly all physical pleasures; fourth, that it is the next step to death. Of each of these reasons, if you will allow me, let us examine the force and justice separately.

6. OLD AGE WITHDRAWS US FROM ACTIVE EMPLOYMENTS. From which of them? Do you mean from those carried on by youth and bodily strength? Are there then no old men's employments to be after all conducted by the intellect, even when bodies are weak? So then Q. Maximus did nothing; nor L. Aemilius – our father, Scipio, and my excellent son's father-in-law! So with other old men – the Fabricii, the Guru and Coruncanii – when they were supporting the State by their advice and influence, they were doing nothing! To old age Appius Claudius had

the additional disadvantage of being blind; yet it was he who, when the Senate was inclining towards a peace with Pyrrhus and was for making a treaty, did not hesitate to say what Ennius has embalmed in the verses:

Whither have swerved the souls so firm of yore?
Is sense grown senseless? Can feet stand no more?

And so on in a tone of the most passionate vehemence. You know the poem, and the speech of Appius himself is extant. Now, he delivered it seventeen years after his second consulship, there having been an interval of ten years between the two consulships, and he having been censor before his previous consulship. This will show you that at the time of the war with Pyrrhus he was a very old man. Yet this is the story handed down to us.

There is therefore nothing in the arguments of those who say that old age takes no part in public business. They are like men who would say that a steersman does nothing in sailing a ship, because, while some of the crew are climbing the masts, others hurrying up and down the gangways, others pumping out the bilge water, he sits quietly in the stern holding the tiller. He does not do what young men do; nevertheless he does what is much more important and better. The great affairs of life are not performed by physical strength, or activity, or nimbleness of body, but by deliberation, character, expression of opinion. Of these old age is not only not deprived, but, as a rule, has them in a greater degree. Unless by any chance I, who as a soldier in the ranks, as military tribune, as legate, and as consul have been employed in various kinds of war, now appear to you to be idle because not actively engaged in war. But I enjoin upon the Senate what is to be done, and how. Carthage has long been harbouring evil designs, and I accordingly proclaim war against her in good time. I shall never cease to entertain fears about her till I hear of her having been levelled with the ground. The glory of doing that I pray that the immortal gods may reserve for you, Scipio, so that you may complete the task begun by your grandfather, now dead more than thirty-two years ago; though all years to come will keep that great man's memory green. He died in the year before my censorship, nine years after my consulship, having been returned consul for the second time in my own consulship. If then he had lived to his hundredth year, would he have regretted having lived to be old? For he would of course not have been practising rapid marches, nor dashing on a foe, nor hurling spears from a distance, nor using swords at close quarters – but only counsel, reason, and senatorial eloquence. And if those qualities had not resided in us seniors, our ancestors would never have called their supreme council a Senate. At Sparta, indeed, those who hold the highest magistracies are in accordance with the fact actually called 'elders'. But if you will take the trouble to read or listen to foreign history, you will find that the mightiest States have been brought into peril by young men, have been supported and restored by old. The question occurs in the poet Naevius's Sport:

> *Pray, who are those who brought your State*
> *With such despatch to meet its fate?*

There is a long answer, but this is the chief point:

> *A crop of brand-new orators we grew,*
> *And foolish, paltry lads who thought they knew.*

For of course rashness is the note of youth, prudence of old age.

7. But, it is said, memory dwindles. No doubt, unless you keep it in practice, or if you happen to be somewhat dull by nature. Themistocles had the names of all his fellow-citizens by heart. Do you imagine that in his old age he used to address Aristides as Lysimachus? For my part, I know not only the present generation, but their fathers also, and their grandfathers. Nor have I any fear of losing my memory by reading tombstones, according to the vulgar superstition. On the contrary, by reading them I renew my memory of those who are dead and gone. Nor, in point of fact, have I ever heard of any old man forgetting where he had hidden his money. They remember everything that interests them: when to answer to their bail, business appointments, who owes them money, and to whom they owe it. What about lawyers, pontiffs, augurs, philosophers, when old? What a multitude of things they remember! Old men retain their intellects well enough, if only they keep their minds active and fully employed. Nor is that the case only with men of high position and great office: it applies equally to private life and peaceful pursuits. Sophocles composed tragedies to extreme old age; and being believed to neglect the care of his property owing to his devotion to his art, his sons brought him into court to get a judicial

decision depriving him of the management of his property on the ground of weak intellect – just as in our law it is customary to deprive a paterfamilias of the management of his property if he is squandering it. Thereupon the old poet is said to have read to the judges the play he had on hand and had just composed – the *Oedipus Coloneus* – and to have asked them whether they thought that the work of a man of weak intellect. After the reading he was acquitted by the jury. Did old age then compel this man to become silent in his particular art, or Homer, Hesiod, Simonides, or Isocrates and Gorgias whom I mentioned before, or the founders of schools of philosophy, Pythagoras, Democritus, Plato, Xenocrates, or later Zeno and Cleanthus, or Diogenes the Stoic, whom you too saw at Rome? Is it not rather the case with all these that the active pursuit of study only ended with life?

But, to pass over these sublime studies, I can name some rustic Romans from the Sabine district, neighbours and friends of my own, without whose presence farm work of importance is scarcely ever performed – whether sowing, or harvesting or storing crops. And yet in other things this is less surprising; for no one is so old as to think that he may not live a year. But they bestow their labour on what they know does not affect them in any case:

He plants his trees to serve a race to come,

as our poet Statius says in his *Comrades*. Nor indeed would a farmer, however old, hesitate to answer any one who asked him for whom he was planting: 'For the immortal gods, whose will it was that I should not merely receive these things from my ancestors, but should also hand them on to the next generation.'

8. That remark about the old man is better than the following:

> If age brought nothing worse than this,
> It were enough to mar our bliss,
> That he who bides for many years
> Sees much to shun and much for tears.

Yes, and perhaps much that gives him pleasure too. Besides, as to subjects for tears, he often comes upon them in youth as well.

A still more questionable sentiment in the same Caecilius is:

> No greater misery can of age be told
> Than this: be sure, the young dislike the old.

Delight in them is nearer the mark than dislike. For just as old men, if they are wise, take pleasure in the society of young men of good parts, and as old age is rendered less dreary for those who are courted and liked by the youth, so also do young men find pleasure in the maxims of the old, by which they are drawn to the pursuit of excellence. Nor do I perceive that you find my society less pleasant than I do yours. But this is enough to show you how, so far from being listless and sluggish, old age is even a busy time, always doing and attempting something, of course of the same nature as each man's taste had been in the previous part of his life. Nay, do not some even add to their stock of learning? We see Solon, for instance, boasting in his poems that he grows old 'daily learning something new'. Or again in my own case, it was only when an old man that I became acquainted with Greek literature, which in fact I absorbed with such avidity – in my yearning to quench, as it were, a long-continued thirst – that I became acquainted with the very facts which you see me now using as precedents. When I heard what Socrates had done about the lyre I should have liked for my part to have done that too, for the ancients used to learn the lyre but, at any rate, I worked hard at literature.

9. Nor, again, do I now MISS THE BODILY STRENGTH OF A YOUNG MAN (for that was the second point as to the disadvantages of old age) any more than as a young man I missed the strength of a bull or an elephant. You should use what you have, and whatever you may chance to be doing, do it with all your might. What could be weaker than Milo of Croton's exclamation? When in his old age he was watching some athletes practising in the course, he is said to have looked at his arms and to have exclaimed with tears in his eyes: 'Ah well! These are now as good as dead.' Not a bit more so than yourself, you trifler! For at no time were you made famous by your real self, but by chest and biceps. Sext. Aelius never gave vent to such a remark, nor, many years before him, Titus Coruncanius, nor, more recently, P. Crassus – all of them learned juris-consults in active practice, whose knowledge of their profession was maintained to their last breath. I am afraid an orator does lose vigour by old age, for his

art is not a matter of the intellect alone, but of lungs and bodily strength. Though as a rule that musical ring in the voice even gains in brilliance in a certain way as one grows old – certainly I have not yet lost it, and you see my years. Yet after all the style of speech suitable to an old man is the quiet and unemotional, and it often happens that the chastened and calm delivery of an old man eloquent secures a hearing. If you cannot attain to that yourself, you might still instruct a Scipio and a Laelius. For what is more charming than old age surrounded by the enthusiasm of youth? Shall we not allow old age even the strength to teach the young, to train and equip them for all the duties of life? And what can be a nobler employment? For my part, I used to think Publius and Gnaeus Scipio and your two grandfathers, L. Aemilius and P. Africanus, fortunate men when I saw them with a company of young nobles about them. Nor should we think any teachers of the fine arts otherwise than happy, however much their bodily forces may have decayed and failed. And yet that same failure of the bodily forces is more often brought about by the vices of youth than of old age; for a dissolute and intemperate youth hands down the body to old age in a worn-out state. Xenophon's Cyrus, for instance, in his discourse delivered on his death-bed and at a very advanced age, says that he never perceived his old age to have become weaker than his youth had been. I remember as a boy Lucius Metellus, who having been created Pontifex Maximus four years after his second consulship, held that office twenty-two years, enjoying such excellent strength of body in the very last hours of his life as not to miss his youth. I need not speak of myself; though that indeed is an old man's way and is generally allowed to my time of life. Don't you see in Homer how frequently Nestor talks of his own good qualities? For he was living through a third generation; nor had he any reason to fear that upon saying what was true about himself he should appear either over vain or talkative. For, as Homer says, 'from his lips flowed discourse sweeter than honey,' for which sweet breath he wanted no bodily strength. And yet, after all, the famous leader of the Greeks nowhere wishes to have ten men like Ajax, but like Nestor: if he could get them, he feels no doubt of Troy shortly falling.

10. But to return to my own case: I am in my eighty-fourth year. I could wish that I had been able to make the same boast as Cyrus; but, after all, I can say this: I am not indeed as vigorous as I was as a private soldier in the Punic war, or as quaestor in the same war, or as consul in Spain, and four years later when as a military tribune I took part in the engagement at Thermopylae under the consul Manius Acilius Glabrio; but yet, as you see, old age has not entirely destroyed my muscles, has not quite brought me to the ground. The Senate-house does not find all my vigour gone, nor the rostra, nor my friends, nor my clients, nor my foreign guests. For I have never given in to that ancient and much-praised proverb:

Old when young
Is old for long.

For myself, I had rather be an old man a somewhat shorter time than an old man *before* my time. Accordingly, no one up to the present has wished to see me, to whom I have been denied as engaged. But, it may be said, I have less strength than either of you. Neither have you the strength of the centurion T. Pontius: is he the more eminent man on that account? Let there be only a proper husbanding of strength, and let each man proportion his efforts to his powers. Such a one will assuredly not be possessed with any great regret for his loss of strength. At Olympia Milo is said to have stepped into the course carrying a live ox on his shoulders. Which then of the two would you prefer to have given to you – bodily strength like that, or intellectual strength like that of Pythagoras? In fine, enjoy that blessing when you have it; when it is gone, don't wish it back – unless we are to think that young men should wish their childhood back, and those somewhat older their youth! The course of life is fixed, and nature admits of its being run but in one way, and only once; and to each part of our life there is something specially seasonable; so that the feebleness of children, as well as the high spirit of youth, the soberness of maturer years, and the ripe wisdom of old age – all have a certain natural advantage which should be secured in its proper season. I think you are informed, Scipio, what your grandfather's foreign friend Masinissa does to this day, though ninety years old. When he has once begun a journey on foot he does not mount his horse at all; when on horseback he never gets off his horse. By no rain or cold can he be induced to cover his head. His body is absolutely free from unhealthy humours, and so he still performs all the duties and functions of a king. Active exercise, therefore, and temperance can preserve some part of one's former strength even in old age.

11. Bodily strength is wanting to old age; but neither is bodily strength demanded from old men. Therefore, both by law and custom, men of my time of life are exempt from those duties which cannot be supported without bodily strength. Accordingly not only are we not forced to do what we cannot do; we are not even obliged to do as much as we can. But, it will be said, many old men are so feeble that they cannot perform any duty in life of any sort or kind. That is not a weakness to be set down as peculiar to old age: it is one shared by ill health. How feeble was the son of P. Africanus, who adopted you! What weak health he had, or rather no health at all! If that had not been the case, we should have had in him a second brilliant light in the political horizon; for he had added a wider cultivation to his father's greatness of spirit. What wonder, then, that old men are eventually feeble, when even young men cannot escape it? My dear Laelius and Scipio, we must stand up against old age and make up for its drawbacks by taking pains. We must fight it as we should an illness. We must look after our health, use moderate exercise, take just enough food and drink to recruit, but not to overload, our strength. Nor is it the body alone that must be supported, but the intellect and soul much more. For they are like lamps: unless you feed them with oil, they too go out from old age. Again, the body is apt to get gross from exercise; but the intellect becomes nimbler by exercising itself. For what Caecilius means by 'old dotards of the comic stage' are the credulous, the forgetful, and the slipshod. These are faults that do not attach to old age as such, but to a sluggish, spiritless, and sleepy old age. Young men are more

frequently wanton and dissolute than old men; but yet, as it is not all young men that are so, but the bad set among them, even so senile folly – usually called imbecility – applies to old men of unsound character, not to all. Appius governed four sturdy sons, five daughters, that great establishment, and all those clients, though he was both old and blind. For he kept his mind at full stretch like a bow, and never gave in to old age by growing slack. He maintained not merely an influence, but an absolute command over his family: his slaves feared him, his sons were in awe of him, all loved him. In that family, indeed, ancestral custom and discipline were in full vigour. The fact is that old age is respectable just as long as it asserts itself, maintains its proper rights, and is not enslaved to any one. For as I admire a young man who has something of the old man in him, so do I an old one who has something of a young man. The man who aims at this may possibly become old in body – in mind he never will. I am now engaged in composing the seventh book of my *Origins*. I collect all the records of antiquity. The speeches delivered in all the celebrated cases which I have defended I am at this particular time getting into shape for publication. I am writing treatises on augural, pontifical, and civil law. I am, besides, studying hard at Greek, and after the manner of the Pythagoreans – to keep my memory in working order – I repeat in the evening whatever I have said, heard, or done in the course of each day. These are the exercises of the intellect, these the training grounds of the mind: while I sweat and labour on these I don't much feel the loss of bodily strength. I appear in court for my friends; I frequently attend the Senate and bring motions before it on my own responsibility, prepared after deep and long reflection. And these I support by my intellectual, not my bodily forces. And if I were not strong enough to do these things, yet I should enjoy my sofa – imagining the very operations which I was now unable to perform. But what makes me capable of doing this is my past life. For a man who is always living in the midst of these studies and labours does not perceive when old age creeps upon him. Thus, by slow and imperceptible degrees life draws to its end. There is no sudden breakage; it just slowly goes out.

12. The third charge against old age is that it LACKS SENSUAL PLEASURES. What a splendid service does old age render, if it takes from us the greatest blot of youth! Listen, my dear young friends, to a speech of Archytas of Tarentum, among the greatest and most illustrious of men, which was put into my hands when as a young man I was at Tarentum with Q. Maximus. 'No more deadly curse than sensual pleasure has been inflicted on mankind by nature, to gratify which our wanton appetites are roused beyond all prudence or restraint. It is a fruitful source of treasons, revolutions, secret communications with the enemy. In fact, there is no crime, no evil deed, to which the appetite for sensual pleasures does not impel us. Fornications and adulteries, and every abomination of that kind, are brought about by the enticements of pleasure and by them alone. Intellect is the best gift of nature or God: to this divine gift and endowment there is nothing so inimical as pleasure. For when appetite is our master, there is no place for self-control; nor where pleasure reigns supreme can virtue hold its ground. To see this more vividly, imagine a man excited

to the highest conceivable pitch of sensual pleasure. It can be doubtful to no one that such a person, so long as he is under the influence of such excitation of the senses, will be unable to use to any purpose either intellect, reason, or thought. Therefore nothing can be so execrable and so fatal as pleasure; since, when more than ordinarily violent and lasting, it darkens all the light of the soul.'

These were the words addressed by Archytas to the Samnite Caius Pontius, father of the man by whom the consuls Spurius Postumius and Titus Veturius were beaten in the battle of Caudium. My friend Nearchus of Tarentum, who had remained loyal to Rome, told me that he had heard them repeated by some old men; and that Plato the Athenian was present, who visited Tarentum, I find, in the consulship of L. Camillus and Appius Claudius.

What is the point of all this? It is to show you that, if we were unable to scorn pleasure by the aid of reason and philosophy, we ought to have been very grateful to old age for depriving us of all inclination for that which it was wrong to do. For pleasure hinders thought, is a foe to reason, and, so to speak, blinds the eyes of the mind. It is, moreover, entirely alien to virtue. I was sorry to have to expel Lucius, brother of the gallant Titus Flamininus, from the Senate seven years after his consulship; but I thought it imperative to affix a stigma on an act of gross sensuality. For when he was in Gaul as consul, he had yielded to the entreaties of his paramour at a dinner-party to behead a man who happened to be in prison condemned on a capital charge. When his brother Titus was Censor, who preceded me, he escaped; but I and Flaccus could not countenance an act of such criminal and abandoned lust, especially as, besides the personal dishonour, it brought disgrace on the Government.

13. I have often been told by men older than myself, who said that they had heard it as boys from old men, that Gaius Fabricius was in the habit of expressing astonishment at having heard, when envoy at the headquarters of King Pyrrhus, from the Thessalian Cineas, that there was a man of Athens who professed to be a 'philosopher', and affirmed that everything we did was to be referred to pleasure. When he told this to Manius Curius and Publius Decius, they used to remark that they wished that the Samnites and Pyrrhus himself would hold the same opinion. It would be much easier to conquer them, if they had once given themselves over to sensual indulgences. Manius Curius had been intimate with P. Decius, who four years before the former's consulship had devoted himself to death for the Republic. Both Fabricius and Coruncanius knew him also, and from the experience of their own lives, as well as from the action of P. Decius, they were of opinion that there did exist something intrinsically noble and great, which was sought for its own sake, and at which all the best men aimed, to the contempt and neglect of pleasure. Why then do I spend so many words on the subject of pleasure? Why, because, far from being a charge against old age, that it does not much feel the want of any pleasures, it is its highest praise.

But, you will say, it is deprived of the pleasures of the table, the heaped-up board, the rapid passing of the wine-cup. Well, then, it is also free from headache, disordered digestion, broken sleep. But if we must grant pleasure something, since we do not find it easy to resist its charms, – for Plato, with happy inspiration, calls pleasure 'vice's bait', because of course men are caught by it as fish by a hook – yet, although old age has to abstain from extravagant banquets, it is still capable of enjoying modest festivities. As a boy I often used to see Gaius Duilius, the son of Marcus, then an old man, returning from a dinner-party. He thoroughly enjoyed the frequent use of torch and flute-player, distinctions which he had assumed though unprecedented in the case of a private person. It was the privilege of his glory. But why mention others? I will come back to my own case. To begin with, I have always remained a member of a 'club' – clubs, you know, were established in my quaestorship on the reception of the Magna Mater from Ida. So I used to dine at their feast with the members of my club – on the whole with moderation, though there was a certain warmth of temperament natural to my time of life; but as that advances there is a daily decrease of all excitement. Nor was I, in fact, ever wont to measure my enjoyment even of these banquets by the physical pleasures they gave more than by the gathering and conversation of friends. For it was a good idea of our ancestors to style the presence of guests at a dinner-table – seeing that it implied a community of enjoyment – a *convivium*, 'a living together'. It is a better term than the Greek words which mean 'a drinking together', or 'an eating together'. For they would seem to give the preference to what is really the least important part of it.

14. For myself, owing to the pleasure I take in conversation, I enjoy even banquets that begin early in the afternoon, and

not only in company with my contemporaries – of whom very few survive – but also with men of your age and with yourselves. I am thankful to old age, which has increased my avidity for conversation, while it has removed that for eating and drinking. But if anyone does enjoy these – not to seem to have proclaimed war against all pleasure without exception, which is perhaps a feeling inspired by nature – I fail to perceive even in these very pleasures that old age is entirely without the power of appreciation. For myself, I take delight even in the old-fashioned appointment of master of the feast; and in the arrangement of the conversation, which according to ancestral custom is begun from the last place on the left-hand couch when the wine is brought in; as also in the cups which, as in Xenophon's banquet, are small and filled by driblets; and in the contrivance for cooling in summer, and for warming by the winter sun or winter fire. These things I keep up even among my Sabine countrymen, and every day have a full dinner-party of neighbours, which we prolong as far into the night as we can with varied conversation.

But you may urge – there is not the same tingling sensation of pleasure in old men. No doubt; but neither do they miss it so much. For nothing gives you uneasiness which you do not miss. That was a fine answer of Sophocles to a man who asked him, when in extreme old age, whether he was still a lover. 'Heaven forbid!' he replied; 'I was only too glad to escape from that, as though from a boorish and insane master.' To men indeed who are keen after such things it may possibly appear disagreeable and uncomfortable to be without them; but to jaded appetites it is pleasanter to lack than to enjoy. However, he cannot be said to lack who does not want: my contention is that not to want is the pleasanter thing.

But even granting that youth enjoys these pleasures with more zest; in the first place, they are insignificant things to enjoy, as I have said; and in the second place, such as age is not entirely without, if it does not possess them in profusion. Just as a man gets greater pleasure from Ambivius Turpio if seated in the front row at the theatre than if he was in the last, yet, after all, the man in the last row does get pleasure; so youth, because it looks at pleasures at closer quarters, perhaps enjoys itself more, yet even old age, looking at them from a distance, does enjoy itself well enough. Why, what blessings are these – that the soul, having served its time, so to speak, in the campaigns of desire and ambition, rivalry and hatred, and all the passions, should live in its own thoughts, and, as the expression goes, should dwell apart! Indeed, if it has in store any of what I may call the food of study and philosophy, nothing can be pleasanter than an old age of leisure. We were witnesses to C. Gallus – a friend of your father's, Scipio – intent to the day of his death on mapping out the sky and land. How often did the light surprise him while still working out a problem begun during the night! How often did night find him busy on what he had begun at dawn! How he delighted in predicting for us solar and lunar eclipses long before they occurred! Or again in studies of a lighter nature, though still requiring keenness of intellect, what pleasure Naevius took in his *Punic War*! Plautus in his *Truculentus* and *Pseudolus*! I even saw Livius Andronicus, who, having produced a play six years before I was born – in the consulship of Cento and Tuditanus – lived till I had become a young man. Why speak of Publius Licinius Crassus's devotion to pontifical and civil law, or of the Publius Scipio of the present time, who within these last few days has been created Pontifex Maximus? And yet I have seen all whom I have mentioned ardent in these pursuits when old men. Then there is Marcus Cethegus, whom Ennius justly called 'Persuasion's Marrow' – with what enthusiasm did we see him exert himself in oratory even when quite old! What pleasures are there in feasts, games, or mistresses comparable to pleasures such as these? And they are all tastes, too, connected with learning, which in men of sense and good education grow with their growth. It is indeed an honourable sentiment which Solon expresses in a verse which I have quoted before – that he grew old learning many a fresh lesson every day. Than that intellectual pleasure none certainly can be greater.

15. I come now to the pleasures of the farmer, in which I take amazing delight. These are not hindered by any extent of old age, and seem to me to approach nearest to the ideal wise man's life. For he has to deal with the earth, which never refuses its obedience, nor ever returns what it has received without usury; sometimes, indeed, with less, but generally with greater interest. For my part, however, it is not merely the thing produced, but the earth's own force and natural productiveness that delight me. For received in its bosom the seed scattered broadcast upon it, softened and broken up, she first keeps it concealed therein (hence the harrowing which accomplishes this gets its name from a word meaning 'to hide'); next, when it has been warmed by her heat and close pressure, she splits it open and draws

from it the greenery of the blade. This, supported by the fibres of the root, little by little grows up, and held upright by its jointed stalk is enclosed in sheaths, as being still immature. When it has emerged from them it produces an ear of corn arranged in order, and is defended against the pecking of the smaller birds by a regular palisade of spikes.

Need I mention the starting, planting, and growth of vines? I can never have too much of this pleasure – to let you into the secret of what gives my old age repose and amusement. For I say nothing here of the natural force which all things propagated from the earth possess – the earth which from that tiny grain in a fig, or the grape-stone in a grape, or the most minute seeds of the other cereals and plants, produces such huge trunks and boughs. Mallet-shoots, slips, cuttings, quicksets, layers – are they not enough to fill anyone with delight and astonishment? The vine by nature is apt to fall, and unless supported drops down to the earth; yet in order to keep itself upright it embraces whatever it reaches with its tendrils as though they were hands. Then as it creeps on, spreading itself in intricate and wild profusion, the dresser's art prunes it with the knife and prevents it growing a forest of shoots and expanding to excess in every direction. Accordingly at the beginning of spring in the shoots which have been left there protrudes at each of the joints what is termed an 'eye'. From this the grape emerges and shows itself; which, swollen by the juice of the earth and the heat of the sun, is at first very bitter to the taste, but afterwards grows sweet as it matures; and being covered with tendrils is never without a moderate warmth, and yet is able to ward off the fiery heat of the sun. Can anything be richer in product or more beautiful to contemplate? It is not its utility only, as I said before, that charms me, but the method of its cultivation and the natural process of its growth: the rows of uprights, the cross-pieces for the tops of the plants, the tying up of the vines and their propagation by layers, the pruning, to which I have already referred, of some shoots, the setting of others. I need hardly mention irrigation, or trenching and digging the soil, which much increase its fertility. As to the advantages of manuring I have spoken in my book on agriculture. The learned Hesiod did not say a single word on this subject, though he was writing on the cultivation of the soil; yet Homer, who in my opinion was many generations earlier, represents Laertes as softening his regret for his son by cultivating and manuring his farm. Nor is it only in cornfields and meadows and vineyards and plantations that a farmer's life is made cheerful. There are the garden and the orchard, the feeding of sheep, the swarms of bees, endless varieties of flowers. Nor is it only planting out that charms: there is also grafting – surely the most ingenious invention ever made by husbandmen.

16. I might continue my list of the delights of country life; but even what I have said I think is somewhat overlong. However, you must pardon me; for farming is a very favourite hobby of mine, and old age is naturally rather garrulous – for I would not be thought to acquit it of all faults.

Well, it was in a life of this sort that Manius Curius, after celebrating triumphs over the Samnites, the Sabines, and Pyrrhus, spent his last days. When I look at his villa – for it is not far from my own – I never can enough admire the man's own frugality or the spirit of the age. As Curius was sitting at his hearth the Samnites, who brought him a large sum of gold, were repulsed by him; for it was not, he said, a fine thing in his eyes to possess gold, but to rule those who possessed it. Could such a high spirit fail to make old age pleasant?

But to return to farmers – not to wander from my own *métier*. In those days there were senators, *i.e.* old men, on their farms. For L. Quinctius Cincinnatus was actually at the plough when word was brought him that he had been named Dictator. It was by his order as Dictator, by the way, that C. Servilius Ahala, the Master of the Horse, seized and put to death Spurius Maelius when attempting to obtain royal power. Curius as well as other old men used to receive their summonses to attend the Senate in their farm-houses, from which circumstance the summoners were called *viatores* or 'travellers'. Was these men's old age an object of pity who found their pleasure in the cultivation of the land? In my opinion, scarcely any life can be more blessed, not alone from its utility (for agriculture is beneficial to the whole human race), but also as much from the mere pleasure of the thing, to which I have already alluded, and from the rich abundance and supply of all things necessary for the food of man and for the worship of the gods above. So, as these are objects of *desire* to certain people, let us make our peace with pleasure. For the good and hard-working farmer's wine-cellar and oil-store, as well as his larder, are always well filled, and his whole farm-house is richly furnished. It abounds in pigs, goats, lambs, fowls, milk, cheese, and honey. Then there is the garden, which the farmers themselves call their 'second flitch'. A zest and flavour is added to all these by hunting and fowling in spare hours. Need I mention the greenery of meadows, the rows of trees, the beauty of vineyard and olive-grove? I will put it briefly: nothing can either furnish necessaries more richly, or present a fairer spectacle, than well-cultivated land. And to the enjoyment of that, old age does not merely present no hindrance – it actually invites and allures to it. For where else can it better warm itself, either by basking in the sun or by sitting by the fire, or at the proper time cool itself more wholesomely by the help of shade or water? Let the young keep their arms then to themselves, their horses, spears, their foils and ball, their swimming baths and running path. To us old men let them, out of the many forms of sport, leave dice and counters; but even that as they choose, since old age can be quite happy without them.

17. Xenophon's books are very useful for many purposes. Pray go on reading them with attention, as you have ever done. In what ample terms is agriculture lauded by him in the book about husbanding one's property, which is called *Oceonomicus*! But to show you that he thought nothing so worthy of a prince as the taste for cultivating the soil, I will translate what Socrates says to Critobulus in that book:

'When that most gallant Lacedaemonian Lysander came to visit the Persian prince Cyrus at Sardis, so eminent for his character and the glory of his rule, bringing him presents from his allies, he treated Lysander in all ways with courteous familiarity and kindness, and, among other things, took him to see a certain park carefully planted. Lysander expressed admiration of the height of the trees and the exact arrangement of their rows in the quincunx, the careful cultivation of the soil, its freedom from weeds, and the sweetness of the odours exhaled from the flowers, and went on to say that what he admired was not the industry only, but also the skill of the man by whom this had been planned and laid out. Cyrus replied: "Well, it was I who planned the whole thing; these rows are my doing, the laying out is all mine; many of the trees were even planted by own hand." Then Lysander, looking at his purple robe, the brilliance of his person, and his adornment Persian fashion with gold and many jewels, said: "People are quite right, Cyrus, to call you happy, since the advantages of high fortune have been joined to an excellence like yours.'"

This kind of good fortune, then, it is in the power of old men to enjoy; nor is age any bar to our maintaining pursuits of every other kind, and especially of agriculture, to the very extreme verge of old age. For instance, we have it on record that M. Valerius Corvus kept it up to his hundredth year, living on his land and cultivating it after his active career was over, though between his first and sixth consulships there was an interval of six and forty years. So that he had an official career lasting the number of years which our ancestors defined as coming between birth and the beginning of old age. Moreover, that last period of his old age was more blessed than that of his middle life, inasmuch as he had greater influence and less labour. For the crowning grace of old age is influence.

How great was that of L. Caecilius Metellus! How great that of Atilius Calatinus, over whom the famous epitaph was placed, 'Very many classes agree in deeming this to have been the very first man of the nation'! The line cut on his tomb is well known. It is natural, then, that a man should have had influence, in whose praise the verdict of history is unanimous. Again, in recent times, what a great man was Publius Crassus, Pontifex Maximus, and his successor in the same office, M. Lepidus! I need scarcely mention Paulus or Africanus, or, as I did before, Maximus. It was not only their senatorial utterances that had weight: their least gesture had it also. In fact, old age, especially when it has enjoyed honours, has an influence worth all the pleasures of youth put together.

18. But throughout my discourse remember that my panegyric applies to an old age that has been established on foundations laid by youth. From which may be deduced what I once said with universal applause, that it was a wretched old age that had to defend itself by speech. Neither white hairs nor wrinkles can at once claim influence in themselves: it is the honourable conduct of earlier days that is rewarded by possessing influence at the last. Even things generally regarded as trifling and matters of course – being saluted, being courted, having way made for one, people rising when one approaches, being escorted to and from the forum, being referred to for advice – all these are marks of respect, observed among us and in other States – always most sedulously where the moral tone is highest. They say that Lysander the Spartan, whom I have mentioned before, used to remark that Sparta was the most dignified home for old age; for that nowhere was more respect paid to years, nowhere was old age held in higher honour. Nay, the story is told of how when a man of advanced years came into the theatre at Athens when the games were going on, no place was given him anywhere in that large assembly

by his own countrymen; but when he came near the Lacedaemonians, who as ambassadors had a fixed place assigned to them, they rose as one man out of respect for him, and gave the veteran a seat. When they were greeted with rounds of applause from the whole audience, one of them remarked: 'The Athenians know what is right, but will not do it.'

There are many excellent rules in our augural college, but among the best is one which affects our subject – that precedence in speech goes by seniority; and augurs who are older are preferred not only to those who have held higher office, but even to those who are actually in possession of *imperium*. What then are the physical pleasures to be compared with the reward of influence? Those who have employed it with distinction appear to me to have played the drama of life to its end, and not to have broken down in the last act like unpractised players.

But, it will be said, old men are fretful, fidgety, ill-tempered, and disagreeable. If you come to that, they are also avaricious. But these are faults of character, not of the time of life. And, after all, fretfulness and the other faults I mentioned admit of some excuse – not, indeed, a complete one, but one that may possibly pass muster: they think themselves neglected, looked down upon, mocked. Besides with bodily weakness every rub is a source of pain. Yet all these faults are softened both by good character and good education. Illustrations of this may be found in real life, as also on the stage in the case of the brothers in the *Adelphi*. What harshness in the one, what gracious manners in the other! The fact is that, just as it is not every wine, so it is not every life, that turns sour from keeping. Serious gravity I approve of in old age, but, as in other things, it must be within due limits: bitterness I can in no case approve. What the object of senile avarice may be I cannot conceive. For can there be anything more absurd than to seek more journey money, the less there remains of the journey?

19. There remains the fourth reason, which more than anything else appears to torment men of my age and keep them in a flutter – THE NEARNESS OF DEATH, which, it must be allowed, cannot be far from an old man. But what a poor dotard must he be who has not learnt in the course of so long a life that death is not a thing to be feared? Death, that is either to be totally disregarded, if it entirely extinguishes the soul, or is even to be desired, if it brings him where he is to exist forever. A third alternative, at any rate, cannot possibly be discovered. Why then should I be afraid if I am destined either not to be miserable after death or even to be happy? After all, who is such a fool as to feel certain – however young he may be – that he will be alive in the evening? Nay, that time of life has many more chances of death than ours. Young men more easily contract diseases; their illnesses are more serious; their treatment has to be more severe. Accordingly, only a few arrive at old age. If that were not so, life would be conducted better and more wisely; for it is in old men that thought, reason, and prudence are to be found; and if there had been no old men, States would never have existed at all. But I return to the subject of the imminence of death. What sort of charge is this against old age, when you see that it is shared by youth? I had reason in the case of my excellent

son – as you had, Scipio, in that of your brothers, who were expected to attain the highest honours – to realize that death is common to every time of life. Yes, you will say; but a young man expects to live long; an old man cannot expect to do so. Well, he is a fool to expect it. For what can be more foolish than to regard the uncertain as certain, the false as true? 'An old man has nothing even to hope.' Ah, but it is just there that he is in a better position than a young man, since what the latter only hopes he has obtained. The one wishes to live long; the other has lived long.

And yet, good heavens! What is 'long' in a man's life? For grant the utmost limit: let us expect an age like that of the King of the Tartessi. For there was, as I find recorded, a certain Agathonius at Gades who reigned eighty years and lived a hundred and twenty. But to my mind nothing seems even long in which there is any 'last', for when that arrives, then all the past has slipped away – only that remains to which you have attained by virtue and righteous actions. Hours indeed, and days and months and years depart, nor does past time ever return, nor can the future be known. Whatever time each is granted for life, with that he is bound to be content. An actor, in order to earn approval, is not bound to perform the play from beginning to end; let him only satisfy the audience in whatever act he appears. Nor need a wise man go on to the concluding 'plaudite'. For a short term of life is long enough for living well and honourably. But if you go farther, you have no more right to grumble than farmers do because the charm of the spring season is past and the summer and autumn have come. For the word 'spring' in a way suggests youth, and points to the harvest to be: the other seasons are suited for the reaping and storing of the crops. Now the harvest of old age is, as I have often said, the memory and rich store of blessings laid up in earlier life. Again, all things that accord with nature are to be counted as good. But what can be more in accordance with nature than for old men to die? A thing, indeed, which also befalls young men, though nature revolts and fights against it. Accordingly, the death of young men seems to me like putting out a great fire with a deluge of water; but old men die like a fire going out because it has burnt down of its own nature without artificial means. Again, just as apples when unripe are torn from trees, but when ripe and mellow drop down, so it is violence that takes life from young men, ripeness from old. This ripeness is so delightful to me, that, as I approach nearer to death, I seem as it were to be sighting land, and to be coming to port at last after a long voyage.

20. Again, there is no fixed borderline for old age, and you are making a good and proper use of it as long as you can satisfy the call of duty and disregard death. The result of this is, that old age is even more confident and courageous than youth. That is the meaning of Solon's answer to the tyrant Pisistratus. When the latter asked him what he relied upon in opposing him with such boldness, he is said to have replied, 'On my old age.' But that end of life is the best, when, without the intellect or senses being impaired, Nature herself takes to pieces her own handiwork which she also put together. Just as the builder of a ship or a house can break them up more easily than any one else, so the nature that knit together the human frame can also

best unfasten it. Moreover, a thing freshly glued together is always difficult to pull asunder; if old, this is easily done.

The result is that the short time of life left to them is not to be grasped at by old men with greedy eagerness, or abandoned without cause. Pythagoras forbids us, without an order from our commander, that is God, to desert life's fortress and outpost. Solon's epitaph, indeed, is that of a wise man, in which he says that he does not wish his death to be unaccompanied by the sorrow and lamentations of his friends. He wants, I suppose, to be beloved by them. But I rather think Ennius says better:

> *None grace me with their tears, nor weeping loud*
> *Make sad my funeral rites!*

He holds that a death is not a subject for mourning when it is followed by immortality.

Again, there may possibly be some sensation of dying and that only for a short time, especially in the case of an old man: *after* death, indeed, sensation is either what one would desire, or it disappears altogether. But to disregard death is a lesson which must be studied from our youth up; for unless that is learnt, no one can have a quiet mind. For die we certainly must, and that too without being certain whether it may not be this very day. As death, therefore, is hanging over our head every hour, how can a man ever be unshaken in soul if he fears it?

But on this theme I don't think I need much enlarge: when I remember what Lucius Brutus did, who was killed while defending his country; or the two Decii, who spurred their horses to a gallop and met a voluntary death; or M.

Atilius Regulus, who left his home to confront a death of torture, rather than break the word which he had pledged to the enemy; or the two Scipios, who determined to block the Carthaginian advance even with their own bodies; or your grandfather Lucius Paulus, who paid with his life for the rashness of his colleague in the disgrace at Cannae; or M. Marcellus, whose death not even the most bloodthirsty of enemies would allow to go without the honour of burial. It is enough to recall that our legions (as I have recorded in my *Origins*) have often marched with cheerful and lofty spirit to ground from which they believed that they would never return. That, therefore, which young men – not only uninstructed, but absolutely ignorant – treat as of no account, shall men who are neither young nor ignorant shrink from in terror? As a general truth, as it seems to me, it is weariness of all pursuits that creates weariness of life. There are certain pursuits adapted to childhood: do young men miss them? There are others suited to early manhood: does that settled time of life called 'middle age' ask for them? There are others, again, suited to that age, but not looked for in old age. There are, finally, some which belong to old age. Therefore, as the pursuits of the earlier ages have their time for disappearing, so also have those of old age. And when that takes place, a satiety of life brings on the ripe time for death.

21. For I do not see why I should not venture to tell you my personal opinion as to death, of which I seem to myself to have a clearer vision in proportion as I am nearer to it. I believe, Scipio and Laelius, that your fathers – those illustrious men and my dearest friends – are still alive, and

that too with a life which alone deserves the name. For as long as we are imprisoned in this framework of the body, we perform a certain function and laborious work assigned us by fate. The soul, in fact, is of heavenly origin, forced down from its home in the highest, and, so to speak, buried in earth, a place quite opposed to its divine nature and its immortality. But I suppose the immortal gods to have sown souls broadcast in human bodies, that there might be some to survey the world, and while contemplating the order of the heavenly bodies to imitate it in the unvarying regularity of their life. Nor is it only reason and arguments that have brought me to this belief, but the great fame and authority of the most distinguished philosophers. I used to be told that Pythagoras and the Pythagoreans – almost natives of our country, who in old times had been called the Italian school of philosophers – never doubted that we had souls drafted from the universal Divine intelligence. I used besides to have pointed out to me the discourse delivered by Socrates on the last day of his life upon the immortality of the soul – Socrates who was pronounced by the oracle at Delphi to be the wisest of men. I need say no more. I have convinced myself, and I hold – in view of the rapid movement of the soul, its vivid memory of the past and its prophetic knowledge of the future, its many accomplishments, its vast range of knowledge, its numerous discoveries – that a nature embracing such varied gifts cannot itself be mortal. And since the soul is always in motion and yet has no external source of motion, for it is self-moved, I conclude that it will also have no end to its motion, because it is not likely ever to abandon itself. Again, since the nature of the soul is not composite, nor has in it any admixture that is not homogeneous and similar, I conclude that it is indivisible, and, if indivisible, that it cannot perish. It is again a strong proof of men knowing most things before birth, that when mere children they grasp innumerable facts with such speed as to show that they are not then taking them in for the first time, but remembering and recalling them. This is roughly Plato's argument.

22. Once more in Xenophon we have the elder Cyrus on his deathbed speaking as follows: –

'Do not suppose, my dearest sons, that when I have left you I shall be nowhere and no one. Even when I was with you, you did not see my soul, but knew that it was in this body of mine from what I did. Believe then that it is still the same, even though you see it not. The honours paid to illustrious men had not continued to exist after their death, had the souls of these very men not done something to make us retain our recollection of them beyond the ordinary time. For myself, I never could be persuaded that souls while in mortal bodies were alive, and died directly they left them; nor, in fact, that the soul only lost all intelligence when it left the unintelligent body. I believe rather that when, by being liberated from all corporeal admixture, it has begun to be pure and undefiled, it is then that it becomes wise. And again, when man's natural frame is resolved into its elements by death, it is clearly seen whither each of the other elements departs: for they all go to the place from which they came: but the soul alone is invisible alike when present and when departing. Once more, you see that nothing is so like death as sleep. And yet it is in sleepers that souls most clearly reveal their divine nature; for they foresee many events when they are allowed to escape and are left free. This shows what they are likely to be when they have completely freed themselves from the fetters of the body. Wherefore, if these things are so, obey me as a god. But if my soul is to perish with my body, nevertheless do you from awe of the gods, who guard and govern this fair universe, preserve my memory by the loyalty and piety of your lives.'

23. Such are the words of the dying Cyrus. I will now, with your good leave, look at home. No one, my dear Scipio, shall ever persuade me that your father, Paulus, and your two grandfathers, Paulus and Africanus, or the father of Africanus, or his uncle, or many other illustrious men not necessary to mention, would have attempted such lofty deeds as to be remaindered by posterity, had they not seen in their minds that future ages concerned them. Do you suppose – to take an old man's privilege of a little self-praise – that I should have been likely to undertake such heavy labours by day and night, at home and abroad, if I had been destined to have the same limit to my glory as to my life? Had it not been much better to pass an age of ease and repose without any labour or exertion? But my soul, I know not how, refusing to be kept down, ever fixed its eyes upon future ages, as though from a conviction that it would begin to live only when it had left the body. But had it not been the case that souls were immortal, it would not have been the souls of all the best men that made the greatest efforts after an immortality of fame.

Again, is there not the fact that the wisest man ever dies with the greatest cheerfulness, the most unwise with the least? Don't you think that the soul which has the clearer and longer sight sees that it is starting for better things, while the soul whose vision is dimmer does not see it? For my part, I am transported with the desire to see your fathers, who were the object of my reverence and affection. Nor is it only those whom I knew that I long to see; it is those also of whom I have been told and have read, whom I have myself recorded in my history. When I am setting out for that, there is certainly no one who will find it easy to draw me back, or boil me up again like second Pelios. Nay, if some god should grant me to renew my childhood from my present age and once more to be crying in my cradle, I would firmly refuse; nor should I in truth be willing, after having, as it were, run the full course, to be recalled from the winning-crease to the barriers. For what blessing has life to offer? Should we not rather say what labour? But granting that it has, at any rate it has after all a limit either to enjoyment or to existence. I don't wish to depreciate life, as many men and good philosophers have often done; nor do I regret having lived, for I have done so in a way that lets me think that I was not born in vain. But I quit life as I would an inn, not as I would a home. For nature has given us a place of entertainment, not of residence.

Oh glorious day when I shall set out to join that heavenly conclave and company of souls, and depart from the turmoil and impurities of this world! For I shall not go to join only those whom I have before mentioned, but also my son Cato, than whom no better man was ever born, nor one more conspicuous for piety. His body was burnt by me, though mine ought, on the contrary, to have been burnt by him; but his spirit, not abandoning, but ever looking back upon me, has certainly gone whither he saw that I too must come. I was thought to bear that loss heroically, not that I really bore it without distress, but I found my own consolation in the thought that the parting and separation between us was not to be for long.

It is by these means, my dear Scipio, – for you said that you and Laelius were wont to express surprise on this point, – that my old age sits lightly on me, and is not only not oppressive but even delightful. But if I am wrong in thinking the human soul immortal, I am glad to be wrong; nor will I allow the mistake which gives me so much pleasure to be wrested from me as long as I live. But if when dead, as some insignificant philosophers think, I am to be without sensation, I am not afraid of dead philosophers deriding my errors. Again, if we are not to be immortal, it is nevertheless what a man must wish – to have his life end at its proper time. For nature puts a limit to living as to everything else. Now, old age is as it were the playing out of the drama, the full fatigue of which we should shun, especially when we also feel that we have had more than enough of it.

This is all I had to say on old age. I pray that you may arrive at it, that you may put my words to a practical test.